CRYPTOCURRENCY AND BLOCKCHAIN FOR EVERYONE

CRYPTOCURRENCY AND BLOCKCHAIN FOR EVERYONE

Shreeram Iyer
and
Sridhar Seshadri

EMBASSY BOOKS
www.embassybooks.in

First Indian Edition,
Published in 2025 by:
Embassy Book Distributors
120, Great Western Building, Maharashtra Chamber of
Commerce Lane, Fort, Mumbai 400 023, India
Tel: (+9122) -30967415, 22819546
Email: info@embassybooks.in
www.embassybooks.in

ISBN: 978-81-19727-44-5

Distribution Centres:
Mumbai, Ahmedabad, Bangalore, Kolkata, Chennai, Hyderabad, New Delhi, Pune

Cover Design by Rishikumar Thakur for Embassy Book Distributors

Printed & bound in India by Repro India Ltd., Navi Mumbai

Table of Contents

Introduction

These days, **crypto and blockchain** have become hot topics everywhere. Country presidents discuss them, and the media covers them relentlessly. Social media is buzzing with discussions, debates, and speculation.

Sooner or later, you start wondering—**does my friend know something about Bitcoin and just isn't telling us?** And that thought lingers.

You usually don't make it your business to keep up with every new trend, but at the same time, you don't want to be one of those people who get left behind while the rest of the world moves on—sometimes making a fortune in the process.

That's exactly what happened with the **internet boom** back in the day. Those who understood it early built empires. **Crypto and blockchain are shaping up to be that next big wave.** You've got to get on board.

We get it because **we were there right from the beginning.**

Shreeram and I explored **Bitcoin and blockchain in 2010**, long before they became mainstream conversations. At the time, they were just an underground movement, a digital experiment with potential. We dove in, researching everything we could, geeking out over the technology, its implications, and the **future it could shape.**

We started writing about it on **blogs, forums, and social media,** and before we knew it, people began reaching out with questions—lots and lots of questions.

Over time, we noticed patterns. We saw what people were truly curious about, what confused them, and what **they really needed to understand** about blockchain and crypto. That's when we realised **we needed to put everything together in one place.**

That's how this book came to life.

Inside, we cover the **ins and outs** of **crypto and blockchain**, including:

- **The Blockchain Revolution** – How this technology is reshaping **finance, security, and the internet** as we know it.

- **Security in the Crypto World** – The biggest mistakes that could cost you your **digital fortune** (and how to avoid them).

- **The Power of Smart Contracts** – How **self-executing code** eliminates middlemen and makes transactions faster.

- **The Rise of NFTs** – Why people spend millions on **digital art**—and whether it's a bubble or the **future of ownership.**

- **Finance (DeFi)** – How banks are being replaced by **code,** and what that means for your money.

- **Surviving Crypto Volatility** – Why prices swing wildly and how to protect yourself from **massive losses.**
- **The Ethics and Sustainability Debate** – Is crypto **bad for the environment,** or is that just a myth?
- **What's Next for Crypto?** – The future of digital currency, regulation, and **mass adoption.**

It doesn't matter if this is your first time exploring this world or if you already have some experience. Whether you're a **beginner, an enthusiast, or even a professional investor,** this book will **equip you with everything you need to know—in record time.**

So, what are you waiting for?

Let's dive in.

Part 1:
The Foundations of Cryptocurrency

To start, we will look at things that are an absolute must to know for anyone interested in cryptocurrencies.

Chapter 1

Understanding Cryptocurrencies

So, what are cryptocurrencies, really?

The definition is a bit technical, but basically, it is a type of decentralised, peer-to-peer, pseudonymous digital money that relies on cryptography to secure transactions.

That sounds like alien-speak, so let us explain the properties to you. Cryptocurrencies are:

- **Digital**: In other words, this type of money exists only as computer code. You'll never find any physical versions of it anywhere. For example, you may have seen physical representations of Bitcoins in images online, but none are real.

- **Decentralised**: In many countries, central banks have always been the institutions responsible for controlling the issuance and supply of a particular currency.

  That type of money has always had a name - ***fiat currency***.

That's not the case with cryptocurrencies.

Instead, the power is given to the people. So, the participants in a given cryptocurrency network run the program that keeps the monetary system in check.

- **Peer to peer**: Guys from the computing world will easily relate to this term, but we'll simplify it. A peer-to-peer network is a special network where the client computers (the devices we use—like laptops, phones, or tablets—to connect to other computers /servers) communicate directly with each other.

  So, if we had a laptop and wanted to send a file to someone else, we would send it directly to them. Easy, right?

  Traditionally, networks have always involved a central server. So, we would send the file to a server first, and the other person would access the file from the server.

It works the same way with crypto. (Traditionally, networks relied on a central server. You would send a file to the server, and the other person would download it from there. With crypto, it's different. Instead of a central server, it often uses a decentralised system where everyone has a copy of the data.)

The essence of peer-to-peer is that you can send money directly to a recipient anywhere in the world without any intermediaries, such as banks and other go-betweens, getting involved in the process.

As we'll later see, this is a revolutionary concept.

- **Pseudonymous**: With the way things are, banks know practically everything about you. After all, when you open an account with them, you provide all private information.

  So, when you send money (or receive it), everyone in authority knows what you've done.

  And that can be a problem.

  Who's to say that someone in power can't abuse that knowledge? You are extending a lot of trust to people who, at some point, may be driven by selfish desires.

  For example, there have been stories of bank employees collaborating with criminals to rob individuals. And possibly that is why, when you call your bank's customer care, the automated waiting tone advises you not to share your OTP or any critical bank details with a customer care agent. With crypto, yes, the network keeps records of transactions, so people can follow a money trail. However, accounts are identified only by a string of numbers and letters. That's all that people see.

  Plus, when you create a wallet, you don't give away personally identifiable information. If you are extra careful, you can stay anonymous.

- **Secured by cryptography**: Cryptography refers to the art of secret writing. It has existed forever, even before computer technology, but in the case of crypto, the tech is used to secure transactions so unauthorised people can't access other people's money.

Are you feeling a little less confused about cryptocurrencies?

Cool!

That said, today, there are several cryptocurrencies. At the time of this writing, the number has exceeded 5,000. And new ones keep being launched all the time.

But there's one crypto that has gained everyone's attention. And it's the one that started all this stuff.

Bitcoin.

We'll look into it to understand the inner workings of cryptocurrencies even more.

Let's go!

About Bitcoin

The History

You've heard the saying "Timing is everything" before, haven't you?

Well, the timing of Bitcoin was as good as anything gets. And it's no wonder cryptocurrency has become so popular.

Let us take you back to 2008, at the height of the financial crisis that brought the world to the brink of utter ruin.

Many people were angry at the banks that caused the mess. When the bailouts came, the public almost lost its mind.

Many people felt that the whole thing was ridiculously unfair. And they were right. But nothing could be done about it.

So, in October of that same year, Satoshi Nakamoto published a whitepaper titled *"Bitcoin: A Peer-to-Peer Electronic Cash System."*

The white paper proposed and outlined the details of how

Bitcoin as a digital currency system might work.

It is assumed that the development of Bitcoin software began right after the whitepaper's publication. In January 2009, the system was ready.

Satoshi mined (the Bitcoin creation process) the first set of Bitcoins and published what is known as the **Genesis block** in the Bitcoin Network.

Then, as any responsible programmer would, he released his work to be reviewed by other programmers and cryptography experts. By the way, these experts were part of the Cypherpunk Movement – a group that started in the 1980s and gained momentum in the 1990s.

Satoshi's code captured many of the ideas that this movement proposed.

This group critiqued the system, including the various ways governments might respond to it, and they worked to improve the code, releasing version 0.2 of the client software system.

Then, in 2010, the system was ready for public use.

So, a Bitcoin user, Laszlo Hanyecz (a programmer), purchased two pizzas for **10,000 BTC on May 22, 2010.** The coins were worth only about **$41**.

This day was commemorated as **Bitcoin Pizza Day**. It spawned the world-famous "**Bitcoin Pizza Index**" – an index that tracks the price of that pizza. we recently checked it, and it sits at an astounding **$1,019,222,537**.

A community started growing around Bitcoin for the rest of the year.

In **February 2011**, Bitcoin price reached par with the US Dollar. The cryptocurrency had now officially arrived on the world stage, and from then on, it rose consistently over the years (with ups and downs, of course).

Today, the currency is worth tens of thousands of dollars, and people regard it as **digital gold**. It has achieved status as both a speculative asset and a tool for wealth preservation.

Sidenote:

Many have debated whether Satoshi Nakamoto is a single individual or a group. The identity behind the name has remained unknown to this day.

Given the sheer scale of the project and the complexity of the ideas that support it, we're inclined to believe that Satoshi Nakamoto represents a group, not just one person.

How It Works

So we know the history.

But how does Bitcoin work in practice?

We'll look at three things – blockchain, mining, and transactions.

Blockchain

Blockchain is the technology that makes Bitcoin operational as a currency.

But it has far-reaching applications beyond just cryptocurrencies.

In fact, some people have argued that Bitcoin was created to demonstrate one of the uses of blockchain technology.

We'll dive into the details of blockchain technology later. For now, understand that for Bitcoin (and other cryptocurrencies), blockchain is simply the decentralised ledger that stores information about transactions in the network.

This ledger is decentralised (or public) because every **node** (device with computing power) in the Bitcoin network stores a copy.

This is done for an important reason - it guarantees the integrity of the information within the ledger.

So, let's say a hacker wanted to alter the information in the ledger somehow, perhaps to make it look like they had more money than they, in fact, did.

Doing so would be nearly impossible because the rest of the computers in the network already store copies of the ledger containing the original transactional information.

So, the ledger that contains contradictory information from the copies in the network is rejected.

Another thing to note is that the name blockchain comes from the fact that the public ledger is organised as a chain of **blocks**. Each block is of a particular size (for Bitcoin, it's about 2 MB) with the ability to store around 4,000 transactions).

Within each block are three critical pieces of data:

- Transaction data
- Timestamps for each transaction
- A cryptographic hash linking the block to the previous one that came before it.

It is crucial to understand that the cryptographic hash is another important security mechanism. As any computer engineering student will tell you, a hash generated from a data set is always unique.

So, if you alter the information within a file or data structure, you cannot produce the same hash.

In a scenario where someone tries to alter a block, the system will reject it because the hash produced will not be the same as the one stored in the next block linking to it.

For these reasons, people consider the blockchain system pretty secure and hacker-proof, especially compared to relational databases used in financial systems.

Mining

What about mining?

When Bitcoin started gaining popularity, stories of people making big money online through mining began making headlines.

So, what is it, and how does it work?

Mining is simply the process through which new Bitcoins are created, and transactions in the network are validated.

We'll explain.

A block of new transactions is added to the public ledger every now and then after the network has verified them.

The computer that gets to do that job gets rewarded with new Bitcoins for providing the crucial service.

But there are many computers in the Bitcoin network, so how does the network decide who gets this privilege?

It's based on a reward system called **Proof of Work (PoW)**. You may have heard of it.

The way it works is that the network provides a mathematical challenge—a cryptographic puzzle, really—and the computers have to compete to solve it.

The node that completes the challenge first gets the privilege to publish the next block of transactions on the public ledger and receive the Bitcoin reward.

It sounds simple, but the reality is that solving that math problem is complex. Really difficult.

To put it into perspective, current estimates show that Bitcoin mining operations consume electric power rivaling that of some countries!

How did we get here?

When Bitcoin was quite young, the math problems required in mining were pretty simple, and even people running home PCs could do it and make some money online.

Other people saw the money, and competition came in.

Also, the value of a currency is, in part, determined by supply and demand forces.

So, to address the problem of too many worthless Bitcoins circulating in the system, Satoshi programmed the system to ensure that only **21 million Bitcoins** will ever exist.

It sounds genius, but it's another problem if people arrive at that number too fast (or quickly). After all, gold, which used to be a stable form of money in the old days, was never easy to mine. That's why it was scarce.

So, the Bitcoin algorithm has been designed to make the mining process progressively more difficult by complicating the math problem computers must solve.

Also, the system cuts the reward given to miners by half every few years – a process called **halving**.

This is one of the reasons why average people can barely do any Bitcoin mining today.

The Proof of Work system makes it prohibitively expensive. Only rich people (or corporations) who can organise massive operations with insane computing power can afford to do so and make it economically sustainable.

Transactions

Now that you understand blockchain and the mining process, let's look at how transactions typically occur.

Imagine you want to send some money to someone. Jiya, perhaps.

What would you do?

The first thing we would suggest is that you open what is called a **Bitcoin Wallet**.

This digital wallet is no different from the ones you are already used to – like your mobile money or PayPal.

It only takes a few minutes to open one, and you can create one such wallet at a place like CoinBase, which also doubles as a cryptocurrency exchange.

What is a cryptocurrency exchange, you ask?

It's a location on the internet that allows you to convert fiat currency into crypto and vice versa.

So, you can head up there and trade in your $100 or any other amount for whatever amount of Bitcoin they are worth, depending on the prevailing market prices.

As we write this, the price of one Bitcoin is **$91,278.**

So, how are you supposed to get any Bitcoin for just **$100?**

That amount is ridiculously low.

The answer is that exchanges allow you to buy **fractional** amounts of a particular security.

After you've exchanged your dollars for Bitcoin, the amount will be credited to your wallet, and you'll be free to start transacting with it.

So what do you do next?

An important thing to note about every Bitcoin wallet owner is that the account comes with three important pieces of information vital to transacting funds.

They are:

- **Wallet Address**: This long string of text and numbers helps uniquely identify your wallet in the Bitcoin network. It is no different from a bank account number.

  Suppose someone wishes to send you money in the Bitcoin network. In that case, this address helps them deposit the money in your account.
- **Public key**: This cryptographic code confirms that you own a particular wallet. Consider it a secondary check that keeps you from sending money to the wrong wallet address.
- **Private key**: This is a cryptographic code that lets you access the funds that are stored in your wallet. It's like a password or PIN that enables you to log into your Bitcoin wallet.

So, this is how it works: to send money to Jiya, you must ask for their wallet address and public key.

Once you have it, you would key the information into your wallet software, instructing it to send a specific amount of Bitcoin to Jiya's wallet.

The software would then broadcast the message across the entire Bitcoin network so every node can verify the authenticity of the request.

Remember, the public ledger contains a record of every transaction that ever took place in the Bitcoin network. So, at any given moment, the network nodes always know the existing balance on each Bitcoin wallet.

This design ensures that a fraudulent transaction is next to impossible.

After the nodes confirm that your request is legitimate, your account is debited, and Jiya's account is credited the amount of Bitcoin you specified.

Then, the transaction is added to a block of other transactions that recently took place and awaits publication on the ledger by the computer that wins the Proof of Work Challenge.

Got it?

Great!

Now that you are familiar with the basics of crypto and how it works, let's look at why this technological innovation is important for everyone.

We'll see you in the next chapter.

Chapter 2

Why Are Cryptocurrencies Important?

So why would Janes and Jones and we care about cryptocurrencies?

What good do they bring into our lives that should make us give a damn and maybe invest our hard-earned money?

We've got a few reasons for you.

1. They Are Decentralised

Okay, so we know what a decentralised currency is, but why does that matter?

Think about all the potential problems that come with a centralised currency.

First, you are placing your trust in your government to issue and control the supply of the currency.

It sounds good to put someone in charge, but we humans have been known to get greedy. Who's to say that someone high up in power who often calls the shots won't print enough money to buy all the goodies that life can afford while the rest of us pick up the bill?

There are times when economic hardships hit – like during **the Covid-19 pandemic and the housing crisis in 2008**.

Governments typically offer stimulus packages to help their citizens weather the storm. Economists call this kind of thing **quantitative easing**. Still, it's all about printing money to fund essential programs to support the economy.

The problem is that when the crisis is eventually averted, the purchasing power of the underlying currency is usually much lower because more notes are circulating through the economy than was previously the case.

That's why some experts argue that government stimulus packages do more harm than good and should be avoided altogether.

Also, think about the big banks and financial institutions at the beating heart of our economies.

Whether we like it or not, corporate giants have a big say in what happens with our money. They always charge hefty transaction fees and can suspend your transaction at any time if they don't like what you are buying.

Did we also mention that they give the government *carte blanche* to freeze your account whenever it feels like it?

When you put all these headaches into perspective, having a decentralised currency no one controls, is a Godsent.

We can deal with each other directly and cut out unnecessary influences.

And when hardships hit, we work with better strategies instead of resorting to ridiculous shortcuts that dilute our currencies' value.

2. Financial Inclusion

It's sad to realise that even in these modern times, a whopping 1.4 billion people have no access to traditional banking services.

The World Bank refers to these people as the unbanked population segment.

But why is there such a large number?

Who knows? Perhaps the traditional banking world has some pretty high standards, and some people can't meet them.

Cryptocurrencies remove those silly barriers.

Suppose you have a smartphone and an internet connection. In that case, you can open a Crypto wallet in minutes and get ready to start transacting.

Simple as that.

Why should it be more complicated?

This is a compelling innovation, especially in developing countries where traditional banking institutions are rife with corruption and government control.

3. They Guarantee Transparency and Security

Where money is involved, transparency is a good policy.

And the issue of security goes without saying.

Traditionally, it has always been a challenging mix to achieve until now.

Crypto transactions are transparent because they are always recorded on a public ledger that anyone can see.

So, if anyone wanted to follow a money trail and know the truth about what happened, they should have an easy time.

Now, transparency doesn't mean much if someone can manipulate the records somehow to achieve a particular desired outcome. But that's nearly impossible with Crypto.

We've looked into this issue. The fact that the blockchain is designed to verify the public ledger at any given time means that someone changing records and succeeding at their attempt is almost impossible.

Even the blocks are designed with cryptographic hashes to ensure no one can alter anything and that the network still accepts it.

These qualities (security and transparency) give crypto a broad appeal, especially in sectors where trust is crucial – like supply chain management, where tracking origins is essential.

4. They Bolster Innovation

As we'll see later in this book, the technology that powers Crypto (blockchain) isn't just about money. Money is just one of its many applications.

Several groundbreaking technologies are currently in development, thanks to blockchain.

Here are just some highlights:

- There are **smart contracts** that run on platforms like Ethereum. These are basically self-executing contracts that have terms written directly into the code.

  They can help automate things like payments, legal agreements, and insurance claims without involving intermediaries.
- In healthcare, patient records can be stored more securely.

- The technology can easily track goods across the global supply chain in logistics.
- In government, more secure voting systems that avoid election fraud can be developed.

These developments can push us towards greater efficiency and improve life.

5. They Can Transform the Global Economy

Crypto can reshape the world economy in the following ways:

- We can have tokenised assets like real estate, art, or company shares traded on blockchain platforms, making them accessible to everyone.
- Decentralised Finance (**DeFi**) can allow people to borrow money, lend it, or even earn interest on digital assets without involving financial intermediaries.
- Cryptocurrency can hedge against inflation for countries that are almost facing financial ruin. For example, when the hyperinflation hit in Venezuela, people took refuge in Bitcoin. They used it as a lifeline because their currency almost lost all its value.

  This type of thing is normally called **fleeing to safety**, and historically, people have always preferred gold for such moves. But times are now changing.

  So, you can see why Bitcoin is slowly gaining the term **digital gold**.

Chapter 3

Altcoins and Stablecoins

But what about altcoins and stablecoins?

Nowadays, it's hard to converse intelligently with anyone about crypto without hearing those phrases at least once.

Altcoins refer to coins other than Bitcoin. The word comes from putting together to phrases – ***alternative*** and ***coins***. So, really, altcoins are just alternative crypto coins.

Remember, Bitcoin was the first cryptocurrency to come onto the world stage.

But right after it became popular, people started poking holes in it (as people would typically do with anything), trying to identify shortcomings and weaknesses.

Soon enough, people started getting other ideas about how things could be done better or differently.

For example, Bitcoin can process only around seven transactions per second. That rate is relatively slow for a network that is supposed to be widely adopted by billions of people worldwide. Compare that with a card network like Visa, which can process thousands of transactions per second, and you'll see what we mean.

That is one of the reasons why an altcoin like Monero was developed – to guarantee the speed of transactions.

Another problem had to do with power consumption. As we've already pointed out, it's not unusual for Bitcoin miners to consume more power than some countries.

Many people feel that that consumption rate is quite wasteful, even absurd.

That's why some coins were developed to rely on different methods of mining new coins or verifying transactions – like ***Proof of Importance*** (POI), which we'll discuss later.

So, How Many Altcoins Exist?

No one is quite sure.

Estimates reveal tens of thousands of altcoins at the time of this writing.

Plus, new altcoins are introduced to the public every now and then. At the same time, many die very quickly, either because they were scams or because the community/developers that supported them lost interest in them.

So, the market is always in constant flux.

A more reasonable question to ask yourself is…

What Kinds of Altcoins Exist?

We can group all altcoins in existence into the following categories:

- Payment tokens
- Security tokens

- Utility tokens
- Meme coins
- Governance tokens
- Stablecoins

We know what you are thinking.

What in the world are **tokens**, and why are we referring to alternative cryptocurrencies that way?

Allow us to explain.

- Tokens are digital assets that are built on a particular blockchain.
- Tokens can either be native or secondary in a particular blockchain.
- For example, Bitcoin is the native token in its blockchain. In other blockchains like Ethereum, you have tokens like USDC, CryptoPunks, and others.

If all this feels confusing, consider this: Imagine a blockchain as an operating system like Windows. Windows comes with native apps like Notepad and the Calculator, which are like native tokens.

However, other third-party apps, such as Opera browser, can be developed and installed in Windows. These are similar to the secondary tokens we've been talking about.

Feeling a lot less confused?

Okay then. Let's discuss the various types of tokens in the crypto world.

Payment Tokens

First, there are payment tokens.

These crypto coins are designed to be used as a medium of exchange or a store of value, pretty much like Bitcoin.

Examples of payment tokens include things like Litecoin (LTC), Dash (DASH), and Bitcoin Cash (BCH).

Security Tokens

These tokens have been designed to represent ownership in tangible world assets, such as stocks, bonds, real estate, precious metals, et cetera.

Issuers of security tokens achieve this tokenisation by transparently holding actual securities in reserves.

If you can think of having digital representations of traditional assets, security tokens are it.

Because security tokens represent regulated securities, the SEC would also need to regulate them.

Examples of security tokens include Polymath (POLY) and tZERO (TZROP).

Utility Tokens

Have you used certain platforms where access to certain features or services requires you to purchase certain unique points?

A service we commonly use that does this kind of thing is Copyscape – a software that helps you check any piece for traces of plagiarism. You probably know what we're discussing if you are a video gamer. You can purchase redeemable points that can help you unlock certain aspects of a particular game. Well, utility tokens are based on the same idea. They allow you, as the holder, to pay and access particular services or features within a platform that's been built on a blockchain. Binance Coin (BNB), Filecoin (FIL), and Chainlink (LINK) are all examples of utility tokens.

Meme Coins

We swear to God the crypto world is nothing if not magnanimous.

Who would've thought a time would come when a public figure, imagine Madonna or Taylor Swift, could launch a coin representing their personality and build a community of fans around it?

And, when someone in that community felt they could cash in on the excitement and euphoria of those who came before them, they traded their coins for what they were worth and made a tidy sum in the process.

But it's not just celebrities who can create meme coins. Some meme coins are based on silly jokes, viral videos, and crazy internet sensations. You merely have to look at the word meme to understand what we're about here.

That's exactly what is happening these days.

The latest case we've heard of is Donald Trump's **$Trump meme coin,** which was developed on the Solana platform. At this time, it's already worth billions, and everybody is going absolutely nuts about it.

The problem with meme coins, as we see it, is that they are

purely speculative instruments with no intrinsic value.

Sometimes, we see them as nothing but pure scams designed to allow early investors, most of whom are the insiders, to cash in on the naiveté and stupidity of others who believe in a quick payday.

Investing in them is no different than participating in a crazy bubble, where you are hoping to buy and hold just so you can pass on the bag to someone who believes they can milk the market too and dump it on someone else.

At some point, someone will doubt the value of what's being offered at a ridiculous price, and everything will unravel from there.

Examples of popular meme coins include the likes of Dogecoin (DOGE), Book of Meme (BOME), Popcat (POPCAT), and Dogs (DOGS).

Governance Tokens

Governance tokens are a special type of utility token that is native to a particular blockchain.

They allow the holders to have certain rights or privileges within that blockchain.

For example, they may allow the holder to have specific voting rights or have a say in a decentralised autonomous organisation (DAO).

Examples of governance tokens include Aave (AAVE), Aragon (ANT), and Dash (DASH).

Now, there's one class of altcoins that's so significant it deserves a discussion of its own – Stablecoins.

What are Stablecoins?

Despite everything we've said about cryptocurrencies, do you want to know the most significant problem they all face? An issue that plagues even Bitcoin – the granddaddy of them all?

It's simply this: they are all volatile as hell.

What do we mean when we speak of volatility?

We mean that their prices go up and down like a mad horse, making them unreliable.

If you buy Bitcoin or some other cryptocoin today, the price could be different even before you go to bed.

And the reason it happens is simple – insufficient liquidity. When not many people participate in a particular financial market, you can expect its price to be unstable.

As we write this, few people have bought into cryptocurrencies as a worthy store of value or investment.

Despite their popularity in both mainstream and social media, crypto still represents a niche market yet to be inducted into the investment hall of fame the way traditional asset classes like stocks, bonds, CFDs (contract for difference), et cetera have.

Look at it this way: if you were a businessperson and someone offered you money in exchange for your widgets, what would you rather receive? Fiat currency or Bitcoin?

We would wager that fiat currency would be your choice. Bitcoin might sound exciting, but what assurances do you have about its price stability? What if the payment you receive is worth much less tomorrow?

With most fiat currency, you don't face such a problem. Unless your country is facing runaway inflation, the prices of most currencies typically hold steady in the interbank market, making them ideal for day-to-day transactions.

Some financial sleuths saw this problem and decided to do something about it.

That's when they introduced stablecoins.

Stablecoins are a type of cryptocurrency designed to sidestep volatility and hold steady in value, making them an ideal choice for typical transactions.

How do the issuers achieve this?

The trick is holding traditional assets such as fiat currency, precious metals, and commodities as collateral. In so doing, the underlying cryptocurrency tracks the asset price that backs it.

Based on collateral, there are four types of stablecoins, namely:

Fiat-Collateralised Stablecoins

Here, the name gives away the goods.

This type of stablecoin is typically backed by a fiat currency held in reserves.

For example, Tether (USDT) is a stablecoin backed by the US Dollar. So is TrueUSD (TUSD). So, their value usually is at par with the US Dollar.

It's no wonder Tether already has a market cap of $142 billion, making it the third-largest cryptocurrency.

Commodity-Backed Stablecoins

The issuers of this type of stablecoins typically invest in commodities such as gold, silver, oil, and so on.

In doing so, they offer currencies whose value is pegged to these commodities.

A good example is Tether Gold (XAUt), a cryptocurrency backed by gold reserves.

Crypto-collateralised Stablecoins

Other cryptocurrencies back these types of stablecoins.

Yeah, we know. It's ridiculous. But there's a good reason why people would think they would hold some value.

Unlike other cryptos, these are typically over-collateralised. In other words, they hold other cryptos in reserve but in excessive amounts compared to what the objective market would indicate.

It's not uncommon to find a 1:2 ratio. Every stablecoin issued is backed by at least double the reserve cryptocurrency. This ratio helps instill investor confidence.

Still, because of the way they are structured, crypto-backed stablecoins are more volatile.

But this last category is even more volatile than anything we've discussed.

Algorithmic Stablecoins

This category holds the least stability and credibility of all stablecoins.

The idea is an algorithm works to keep the supply of the

cryptocurrency in check so it doesn't adversely affect the price.

This is similar to how many governments operate today. Most, like the U.S., don't keep gold reserves like they used to.

They print money and require us to rely on the government's faith and credibility to believe that the currency is worth what it says.

It's a slippery slope, but it's worked fine so far.

Now, governments monitor the supply circulating an economy at any moment to keep currency values from falling off a cliff. When the supply is too much, they institute policies that reduce the number of notes going around,

When the supply is too little, they ease borrowing through banks to get more notes into the system.

In reality, the process is a lot more complicated than what we've just described. The details remain with the geniuses who work at the Federal Reserve and Central Banks worldwide. But at least you get the idea.

Because Stablecoins have attracted so much money, governments feel they are systemically important. In other words, the money circulating in them is enough to bring the world financial system to the brink of disaster if something goes wrong.

Therefore, leading governments propose regulating stablecoins like any other financial market to avoid systemic risk.

It hasn't happened yet, but it's something we should expect soon.

Now that you know the fundamentals of cryptocurrencies, we're sure you're eager to get your hands dirty.

After all, what good is it to know all this stuff if you won't get in the game?

Fair enough.

In the next chapter, we will explain how to get started with cryptocurrencies. Sit tight.

Chapter 4

How to Get Started with Cryptocurrencies

So, let's say you are starting out with nothing.

Yes, you've spent time accumulating basic crypto theory and feel proud of yourself. And you should. With what you've learned thus far, you could flaunt what you know at a date or a party, and people will stop to listen.

This is awesome.

Except.

You own no crypto. Not even a little Bitcoin.

What if someone asks how much crypto you own? Everyone knows how valuable Bitcoin is today. Could you even explain what your portfolio looks like?

If not, knowing so much and doing very little about it would be a tragedy.

It indeed would be. And we need to put a stop to it.

Let's go over the steps you need to take to get started with crypto quickly.

Step 1: Setting Up Your Wallet

It all starts with getting a wallet.

You've dealt with some versions of e-wallets in your life, right?

They are everywhere. And even if you haven't operated one, you've at least done some online banking either on your PC or your mobile phone.

Well, with crypto, it's pretty much the same thing.

Crypto wallets allow you to manage your funds in one place. You can check your balance, send money somewhere, and also receive it.

To operate a wallet, you need three key pieces of information, as shared earlier:

- A public address
- A public key
- A private key

A **public address** is unique to everyone in the Bitcoin network. It's a long string of letters and numbers that works like a bank account number.

So, whenever someone needs to send funds to you, you need to give it to them.

Another notable aspect of addresses is that you can have several. There is no limit to how many you can create and store in your wallet.

A public key is closely related to your **public address**. It helps verify that the public address is yours and encrypts the transaction so unauthorised persons cannot tamper with it.

Lastly, there's a **private key**. A private key helps you access your funds and allows you to spend them as you please. It's like having a PIN or password for your mobile wallet.

It's time to consider which type of wallet you should set up. They are not all the same, and it's good to know which type suits you and your situation.

Type 1: Online Wallet

As the name suggests, these are wallets that reside online.

Exchange platforms like **Kraken** and **Coinbase** offer digital crypto wallets, so you can store crypto coins as soon as you purchase them. However, several independent providers offer wallets, too.

For example, we favour *https://www.blockchain.com* for creating an online wallet. It's free and open source, but we are not making any recommendations for you here.

The cool thing about online wallets is that they allow you to access your coins anywhere in the world, provided you have an internet connection.

If you are excited about something like that, you should consider them.

The bad news is that online wallets can be hacked.

In the early days of Bitcoin, many wallet providers became the prime targets of hackers, and big names like Mt. Gox, the leading crypto exchange in the world at the time, made headlines after repeatedly being compromised and untold fortunes stolen.

Security is much better these days, but the risk is always present. We've worked in computing and can confidently tell you that no system is always 100% secure. It's usually a matter of time before someone figures out a way.

Because security is always a big problem online, we wouldn't recommend storing large amounts of crypto in online wallets. Only stash amounts that you need for small expenditures.

If you've got a million dollars in Bitcoin, storing it in an online wallet is nuts. Even if criminals don't get to you, are you okay trusting some third party with that much of your money?

Suppose they end up being the target of an investigation. You could easily have your assets frozen. Wisen up. There are much better options.

Type 2: Mobile Wallet

Online wallets have a close cousin – mobile wallets.

You can access them through an app, meaning you can use them practically anywhere. This is a huge convenience, especially since crypto is slowly becoming a payment method.

Some good mobile crypto wallets include:

- Exodus
- Coinomi
- Zengo
- OKX
- Trust Wallet

Even Coinbase has an app; you might want to check it out.

The trouble with mobile wallets is that you better pray your phone doesn't get damaged, stolen, or infected with malware.

These are potential scenarios in which you risk losing money because someone could look up your keys and empty your accounts.

You can take some security measures, which we'll discuss soon. However, understand that the risk is pretty high.

My advice for this category of wallet is pretty much the same as for the online version: Only carry small amounts of money you need and can afford to lose, and don't take big chances.

Type 3: Desktop Wallets

If you've got a computer, it helps to know that there exist client software designed to serve as wallets.

It's no different from mobile apps. They both fall under an umbrella called software wallets.

We wouldn't say the advantages are anything special. The lack of mobility is, in fact, a disadvantage.

In addition, your computer can become infected with malware, such as **keystroke loggers** and **spyware,** which can help hackers steal your money.

Some people try to circumvent this problem by storing the wallet files on a computer that has never been connected to the Internet.

We suppose that helps transform the computer into a cold wallet. But it's a thin line because computers that have not connected to the Internet are at greater risk of malware infection, as the software isn't updated and patched.

That's another reason we never recommend storing large amounts of money on desktop wallets.

Sidenote: By the way, **cold wallets** refer to wallets that store your keys offline. **Hot wallets** store your keys online.

To feel safe, you need cold wallets, which are either hardware or paper wallets.

Type 4: Hardware Wallets

Hardware wallets are a brilliant invention and are the first type of cold wallet you should consider.

They store your keys on a USB drive, allowing easy retrieval.

You can transact online using them, but the fact that your keys stay offline most of the time makes them cold wallets.

If you are considering storing crypto coins worth significant amounts of money, this is one option, and we highly recommend it.

But, if you are paranoid, a paper wallet is even better.

Type 5: Paper Wallet

So, what is a paper wallet, and how does it work?

It's nothing fancy, really.

If you can create a fresh public address and print out your public and private keys on paper (most paper wallet generators also allow you to create and print a QR code), you've got one.

Here's how that would work in practice:

1. Find a computer that is free of malware or viruses. Ideally, this would be a computer with a newly installed operating system. The idea is that you don't want to risk it by having it connected to the internet. Ever.
2. Use the private mode of your browser to find a crypto wallet generator. Just Google "crypto wallet generators," and you should see some reliable sites. we personally love *https://www.walletgenerator.com*
3. Once the site loads, turn off your internet connection.

Such generators are designed to work perfectly well offline.

4. You should see a function that allows you to generate a new address for the cryptocurrency of your choice. Use it, and you should get a new address and public and private keys. A QR code should be generated right along with them.
5. From there, print the page and keep the paper safe.

Now you have to send funds to that address and store the paper in a safe place where you cannot lose it because losing that paper also means letting go of all your money – for good.

When you want to access your funds, you can use wallet software to scan your QR code and retrieve the keys, which you can then use to access your funds.

A paper wallet is the best option if you have a sizeable fortune you'd like to store as crypto. You can store your money safely for years that way.

Now, here's an important thing to note about crypto paper wallets. You cannot consider them an ultra-safe option anymore once you log onto your wallet online. At that point, they cease to become cold wallets because you've exposed your public and private keys.

That's why we would never recommend this type of wallet for small everyday transactions. Use the other wallets we've discussed for that kind of thing.

If you want to keep your money safe for the foreseeable future, you must create another cold wallet and transfer all your funds there.

Step 2: Acquire Crypto

Okay, you know enough about wallets that you've chosen the ideal option.

Now it's time to load it up.

When it comes to this, you have a few main options:

- You can mine them
- You can exchange them for valuable items
- You can purchase your crypto coins for cash at an exchange
- You can exchange them directly with someone for cash

The first option is unattainable for most average people. It takes way more resources than most people can afford to put on the line so you can safely cross it off your list.

The second one is way more reasonable. If you have something of value that another person wants and may be willing to transact in Bitcoins.

The third option is the one most people rely on – where you exchange fiat currency for crypto coins and vice versa.

And there are three types of exchanges in the cryptocurrency universe:

- There are **Centralised Cryptocurrency Exchanges (CEX)**
- **Decentralised Cryptocurrency Exchanges (DEX)**
- **Hybrid Cryptocurrency Exchanges**

Centralised Cryptocurrency Exchanges (CEX)

A centralised cryptocurrency exchange is no different from a stock exchange and other traditional exchanges you may be aware of.

Here, money is held in escrow by a central trusted entity, doubling down as a match-making service. So essentially, buyers and sellers of a particular crypto coin come together, and the exchange allows them to do business with each other on the platform.

As we write this, several trusted service providers of this type exist. They include:

- Coinbase
- Kraken
- Bittrex
- Gemini

Usually, after you open an account with one of these exchanges, you are assigned a hot wallet where you can deposit your cryptocurrency.

Also, you gain access to their trading platform, which allows you to carry out your intended business.

For example, say you wanted to exchange US dollars for Bitcoin. The perfect way to handle that transaction would be to look for a pair labeled BTC/USD on the platform.

Then, you would click the BUY button on the screen. Effectively, that would allow you to buy Bitcoin while simultaneously selling USD.

Bitcoins would be deposited to your hot wallet, and you

would immediately start seeing the value of whatever amount of Bitcoin you bought calculate itself on screen.

Now, say you wanted to exchange your Bitcoin for USD. In that case, you would click the SELL button.

That would instruct the software to find an order allowing you to sell Bitcoin and buy USD. It's merely the reverse of the previous request.

And that's the way it works with centralised exchanges. But what about decentralised exchanges?

Decentralised Cryptocurrency Exchanges

Many diehard crypto fanatics scoff at the idea of centralised exchanges.

To them, handing power and trust of their money to a central entity undermines the foundations on which cryptocurrencies were built.

For those reasons, decentralised cryptocurrency exchanges emerged.

These exchanges operate a peer-to-peer network that allows people to control their reserves and trade directly with other people of similar interests.

So, if we were to buy bitcoin, we would buy directly from another seller without involving a middleman.

Don't get too excited, though. The trouble with decentralised crypto exchanges is that few people have embraced them. However, that is likely to change with time.

But, in the meantime, the insufficient trading volume in decentralised exchanges means that liquidity is always a big issue.

And you know what that implies?

Large transaction fees can often make trading in a decentralised crypto exchange costly.

Despite all this knowledge, if you still insist on trading in a decentralised exchange, the following places will let you do it:

- Uniswap
- Sushiswap
- Pancakeswap
- 1inch

But then there is another category of exchanges that try to capitalise on the good points of the previous two.

Hybrid Exchanges

Hybrid exchanges were formed to compensate for the weaknesses of centralised and decentralised exchanges, offering people the best of both worlds.

The details are a bit complex, but the idea is that a hybrid network connects centralised elements to decentralised elements, attempting to achieve a healthy mix.

This architecture allows people to access the platform as though they were in a centralised exchange but trade in a peer-to-peer fashion as if they were in a decentralised exchange, recording all transactions on a blockchain.

It's genuinely a next-generation design, and many people are starting to believe that this architecture represents crypto exchanges' future.

Good examples of hybrid exchanges are Qurrex and NEXT. exchange.

But again, adoption is still slow. It may change with time.

All things considered; we would recommend going with centralised exchanges as we wait for the other types of exchanges to catch up.

After that, it's all a matter of securing your coins.

Step 3: Securing Your Crypto

Nobody enjoys losing money. And we can't imagine losing your crypto coins would be fun, either.

Yes, we've covered how you can store coins securely using hardware and paper wallets, but here are some additional tips that can step up your security.

1. Backup Your Wallet

Keep a backup copy of all your keys.

And whenever you create a new address, add it to your backup.

This is no different from keeping a backup of all your files in case something happens. This is the 21st century, after all. Anything can happen.

2. Use Multiple Wallets

Some crypto enthusiasts call this strategy diversifying your wallets.

They mean to say, don't keep all your money in one type of wallet. Store various amounts across different types of wallets.

When you do that, if one wallet is compromised, you don't lose all your money. You can make do with other wallets.

The chances of all your wallets getting compromised are close to zero.

3. Add More Security Levels

With software wallets, you can step up security in the following ways:

- **Use 2-factor authentication**: Check whether your wallet provider offers this option. Essentially, it allows for a double authentication of who you are, which can be done in different ways.
- **Encrypt your wallet**: You can also add an extra layer of security to your wallet. This option allows you to set a password to log into the wallet software before you start carrying out the transaction.
- **Use a strong password**: Merely setting a password is not enough. You have to make sure it's strong. What's a strong password? A strong password is alphanumeric, contains punctuations, and is at least 16 characters long.

  Many password generators online can help you create a secure password that meets the above criteria.

  You can copy the passwords to a safe place to allow them when needed.

4. Keep Your Software Up to Date

This one is also crucial. Whatever you do, keep your wallet software updated to the latest version.

Frequently, bugs get discovered, and security issues get fixed and rolled into updates.

So, when an update notification comes up, don't pass it up.

5. Remember Your Hiding Locations

This one's obvious, but some people screw it up.

If you follow excellent security practices but tend to forget where you store essential details like passwords and keys, then it won't matter.

You could lose everything.

So, don't let it happen.

Moving on to the next section, we'll explore the fundamentals of blockchain technology. You don't want to miss this.

Part 2: Blockchain Basics

Talk to most computer geeks, and they'll tell you that blockchain technology is the fifth evolution of computing.

Why do they say that?

Turns out there are good reasons. And in this part, we are going to look at why.

Chapter 5

Blockchain and How Does It Work?

In the previous part of this book, we took a surface-level look at blockchain.

But we never took a deep dive into its mechanics.

So, let's address that real quick.

Let's start with the definition.

What Is Blockchain?

It's a decentralised digital ledger that keeps records of transactions securely, permanently, and transparently across a distributed network of computers.

That's a pretty technical definition, we know. If you are having a hard time understanding it, don't worry.

This next discussion of its key principles will clear things up for you.

Core Principles of Blockchain

Blockchain technology is unique because it operates on three key principles that distinguish it from other data storage structures.

They are:

- Decentralisation
- Immutability
- Transparency and security

Let's look at each one of them in turn.

Decentralisation

What do we mean when we talk of decentralised?

In computer science, people usually describe a **client-server** architecture when discussing networking.

This design usually allows computers (such as your home desktop computer, laptop, or phone) to communicate with a server when accessing information in a network.

This design has persisted for years and years, ever since the internet was born. And it has always served its purpose.

The problem is that it requires you to trust the central authority that operates and maintains the server. The server stores essential and sensitive data, like your medical information or identity, so you must trust that the operator will not abuse that information.

Blockchain technology implies: "There's no need to have a central party or place trust on anyone. People can safely store information by themselves and verify it, eliminating the need for a central entity."

That is the essence of a **peer–to–peer (P2P)** network. Client computers store information on their own hard drives, making it available to other client computers within the network whenever needed.

The presence of a central server is irrelevant.

If you've used torrent networks to download anything from websites like **The Pirate Bay**, you know what we're talking about.

Torrent networks are classical **P2P** networks that store files on individuals' computers worldwide. They allow anyone to access and download the files, circumventing copyright regulatory frameworks.

No one can take down a torrent network because there's no server to seize. If any server stored all the material found in torrent networks, the FBI would get busy, and they wouldn't last long.

Immutability

When something is immutable, we mean to say that it is unchangeable. It can't be altered.

And that's characteristic of blockchain records.

Once a record has been added to the ledger, no one can change it.

And that happens for two reasons.

First, most computers (over 51%) within the P2P networks must agree that the proposed information is authentic.

And remember, these computers store all the information starting from the first block created in the network, called the **Genesis block**. No detail escapes them.

If all these computers can't agree that the change is authentic, the change will be rejected.

The second reason is that the information within each block

produces a cryptographic hash, essentially a unique identifier for that information – kind of like a fingerprint for that particular block.

With cryptographic hashes, you can't change information within the block without changing the hash it produces.

So, to prevent the rest of the blockchain from rejecting it, you would need to change every other block on it. This is computationally unfeasible, and no one would ever bother.

The longer the blockchain is, the more secure it becomes, making it even less likely that anyone would try to modify it.

Transparency

Transactions happening in a blockchain are visible to anyone in the network.

For example, in the Bitcoin network, everyone can see all the transactions published in the public ledger.

For more private blockchains, every trusted network member can see all the information in the ledger.

Because the information isn't secret, it promotes an element of transparency and trust that is hard to match.

Okay, so now that you understand the core principles of blockchain, how does it operate?

How Blockchain Works

The key to understanding how blockchain works lies in examining its key components:

- Blocks – the data containers
- Chains – the links that secure the records
- Nodes – the computers maintaining the network

Blocks: The Building Units of Blockchain

A block is the most fundamental unit of a blockchain. Each block contains the following pieces of information:

1. Transaction Data

Thus far, we've mainly focused on Bitcoin, so it's easy for you to assume that transaction data means financial information.

And that is partly true.

But that's not the only transaction data that can be stored in a blockchain.

Depending on the purpose of the blockchain or the system it supports, the data can be formatted to also record transactions such as:

- **Smart contract executions**: We'll get to these later, but essentially, know that these are digital agreements hosted on the Ethereum platform.
- **Supply chain updates**: For example, IBM's Foodtrust Blockchain tracks shipments.
- ...and more.

2. Timestamp

This information helps ensure that data is stored in the proper chronological order.

It also helps prevent double-spending, a serious issue where digital assets are spent more than once.

3. Cryptographic Hash

We've talked about how this is a unique fingerprint that identifies a block's contents.

Now, the thing is, every block contains a hash of the block that came before it. This way, the network creates a link that secures all blocks to the Genesis block.

To put all this into context, imagine yourself keeping a diary. Each page of the diary contains the following:

1. **A current date** is like a timestamp for a block's data.
2. **A summary of the day's events**: This is the equivalent of transaction data.
3. **A reference to the previous page**: This is what a hash is all about.

Got it?

Now, if someone got their hands on your diary and tried to edit an entry you made earlier, it means they would also need to change every subsequent page on the damn booklet.

It's crazy to attempt something like that, mainly if the diary contains several pages, so most people don't bother.

Nodes

As we've already said, a node is a computer that connects to a particular network (in this case, the blockchain network).

Nodes in a blockchain network are essential because they **store**, **validate**, and **share** data, ensuring the blockchain remains **decentralised** and **secure**.

What you may not know is that there are three types of nodes:

- Full Nodes
- Light Nodes
- Validator Nodes

Full Nodes

Full nodes are given that name because they store the entire blockchain history, from the most recent to the Genesis block.

Full nodes are typical in public blockchains like Bitcoin and Ethereum.

Light Nodes

Then, light nodes are designed to store only essential blockchain data, never the entire history.

They are great for devices with low storage and need quick verification, such as mobile wallets.

If you are using a crypto wallet on your phone, it would be crazy to imagine it downloads the entire blockchain.

The size of the Bitcoin blockchain is probably several gigabytes by now, and most phones can't handle that.

So, your phone merely operates as a light node.

Validator Nodes

This type of node is common in enterprise blockchains.

With this design, only a select number of network nodes take on the job of storing the entire blockchain and verifying transactions. Doing this helps ensure scalability without compromising security.

A good example of a network that uses a validator is **Ripple**. It relies on validator nodes chosen from a trusted set of computers.

Because it takes this route, Ripple is considered among the fastest cryptocurrencies compared to Ethereum and Bitcoin.

Consensus Mechanisms

You've understood the core structure of blockchain, but have you ever wondered how a particular blockchain decides that a block of transactions is valid and should be added to the existing chain?

Because there's no central authority, all the computers in the network need to agree on the same version of the truth.

It takes a particular set of rules for the distributed nodes to agree on what gets published.

That set of rules is called a **consensus mechanism**, and many of them exist. We'll discuss the most popular ones.

1. Proof of Work (PoW)

We've seen how this works.

Basically, nodes in the blockchain network compete to solve a cryptographic puzzle. The first node to complete the challenge gets the privilege to publish the next block of transactions.

This process is called mining, and in return for providing that service, the node gets rewarded with newly minted cryptocurrency.

This, in essence, is how Bitcoin and Ethereum (before version 2.0) have always worked.

It's a sound enough method, except it faces some problems.

First, it's damn too expensive. Experts estimate that Bitcoin mining exceeds the power consumption of countries like Argentina and the Netherlands.

That's a huge waste, especially when we know we should be conserving energy or making it more available to people so that it becomes cheaper.

We watched a documentary about a town where residents who enjoyed cheap electricity got bills that were more than double the original price simply because a Bitcoin miner set up shop over there and, before long, began competing with the locals over price.

Also, Proof of Work is difficult for most people to achieve simply because it requires expensive hardware that is beyond their reach.

Did we also mention that the transaction processing is painfully slow? The best speed one can hope for in Bitcoin is merely seven transactions per second (TPS), making it unreliable for daily retail payments.

2. Proof Of Stake

Proof of Stake (PoS) was designed to address the issues regarding energy wastage that Bitcoin PoW poses.

Additionally, the transaction speeds are significantly higher, reaching approximately 100,000 Transactions Per Second (TPS).

It all sounds impressive, so what's the trick to achieving that? How does it work?

First, participants stake or lock up their assets as collateral. The reason for doing this is that part of the stake can be forfeited in the event of a fraudulent transaction. This is one way this method tries to curb fraud.

The idea is that the more you stake as collateral in the network, the more likely you'll be assigned the privilege to update the ledger and get a reward.

The reward will either be a newly minted coin or a transaction fee.

This is the new direction that **Ethereum 2.0** (ETH) is taking. **Polkadot** (DOT) and **Cardano** (ADA) are other examples that operate similarly.

As efficient as it sounds, this system has its weaknesses.

For example, you could argue that the system encourages people to hoard coins. After all, the more they stake, the greater the percentage of transactions the node can process.

If that's not an incentive to keep people from spending their coins, we don't know what is.

Proof of Importance (PoI)

A blockchain called the New Economy Movement (NEM) first introduced this method to support the XEM cryptocurrency.

Proof of Importance is remarkably similar to PoS.

Computers are eligible for mining if they have a certain amount of the underlying cryptocurrency vested.

The network then calculates an importance score and assigns it to the particular node. Now, the node can process a block with a size proportional to its importance score.

However, the creators of this model understood PoS's primary shortcoming—it tends to make the rich richer by doing nothing.

PoS addresses that issue by not simply assigning a higher score to nodes hoarding coins.

It considers other variables.

It's not immediately obvious what those variables are, but the idea is to reward the most active network participants and those who contribute the most to the community, not just those who keep coins and sit on them.

So, the more important you are as a node to the network, the more chances you have of mining.

This model, in my opinion, is quite fair.

However, these are not the only consensus models in use. There are other, less popular ones, such as:

Delegated Proof of Stake (DPOS)

DPOS is a more complicated consensus mechanism that solves PoS's shortcomings and ensures fairness.

First, understand that only a select group of delegates (also known as validators) are tasked with validating the transaction. Their number is usually kept fixed, ranging from as little as **21** to as much as **100**.

You might wonder, how do these delegates get chosen?

Well, it's through a democratic process. Sort of.

Here's what we mean:

Step 1: Token holders in a network vote for a trusted group of delegates, who are the **witnesses** or **validators** of the entire network.

In the voting process, the more tokens one holds in the network, the greater their power in the voting process.

Step 2: Once the delegates have been elected, they take turns processing transactions in the network round-robin, so there's fairness.

Step 3: The delegates earn their rewards for processing blocks. They can then redistribute those earnings among voters to encourage participation in the overall network.

This model is more democratic, energy-efficient, and faster (it can process as many as 4,000 transactions per second).

But that's not to imply that it's without shortcomings.

If it hasn't occurred to you already, this system allows for forming a cartel within a network. And that cartel may start acting in ways that are not in everyone's best interests.

But, the likelihood of that happening is quite remote because delegates can be replaced if they act maliciously or fail to perform their duties.

This is the system that has powered platforms such as:

- EOS
- Tron
- VeChain

Proof Of Authority

So far, we've discussed consensus mechanisms that work for public blockchains. However, the uses of blockchain extend well beyond that.

For example, blockchain technology is currently being applied in the business world and government.

Imagine systems that validate supply chain management, logistics, and finance transactions.

Proof of Authority (PoA) is more valuable in places like these and makes more sense.

So, what is it?

PoA is a mechanism where a small, trusted group of pre-approved validators is chosen to verify transactions and create new blocks.

Don't confuse this with DPoS. In DPoS, the network's member nodes vote for the entities trusted to update the blockchain and approve transactions.

In PoA, the entities are handpicked from the very start.

And these aren't just any entities we're talking about. We're talking about businesses, organisations, or individuals with a public image deemed trustworthy.

This is entirely different from other models where we've seen that validators can be, and often are, anonymous.

Anyway, such validators will now take turns verifying transactions and adding them to the blockchain. This is done without any need for competition or mining.

Because trust has been extended to such parties, they are expected to uphold that confidence level. They are not expected to act dishonestly, as that would be grounds for their ruined reputation and subsequent removal from the network.

Business applications favour this type of consensus mechanism because it does not require tokens or mining rewards.

Here are some real-world examples we can think of:

- **VeChain** relies on PoA to track the authenticity of products in sensitive industries like pharmaceuticals and luxury goods, minimising the risk of counterfeits.
- **Binance SmartChain** relies on PoA to provide a platform that supports DeFi applications and Smart contracts.

- Then, Microsoft Azure Blockchain Service helps securely share data using PoA.
- The banking world is exploring ways to use PoA to create **tamper-proof digital identities** to reduce fraud cases.

Now, PoA poses a few problems.

The first is that it creates a **centralisation risk**. Because of how the mechanism works, it creates a scenario where a few entities could control the entire network.

This prospect alone tends to undermine the principles of decentralisation on which blockchain technology was built.

Second, trust must be placed in those few entities that validate and update.

This backward mentality doesn't sound very racy to blockchain enthusiasts.

Most people interested in blockchain are excited by the prospect of a system in which no one needs to trust anyone. In this system, even enemies can do business with each other without worrying about anyone double-crossing the other.

PoA tends to do the exact opposite.

Despite these concerns, we think it's a useful system for private blockchain networks, where some element of trust makes sense, and responsible parties are well-known.

It totally sucks for public blockchains, though.

Proof of Burn

This consensus mechanism is quite weird in the way it works.

Network participants must "burn" or completely destroy their tokens to get mining privileges in the system and validate transactions.

But there's a reason for this apparent madness.

The logic behind destroying token holdings is to demonstrate a long-term commitment to the network. And those who do so deserve special privileges to mine new coins and validate transactions.

But why burn coin holding in the first place?

Besides proving that you are committed to the long-term well-being of the network, this is the mechanism the network uses to keep the total supply of coins in circulation in check and avoid hyperinflation, which could erode their value.

It works in practice because once you join the network, you can send your coins to an **"unspendable burn address."** Once you do that, you effectively remove the coins from circulation entirely.

The more coins you burn that way, the more voting or mining privileges you gain in the system.

This idea of burning coins also helps solve another problem – liquidity runs.

The burning of the coins ensures that people stay in the system for the long haul. Imagine a scenario where people in a PoS system panic. They would quickly dump their coin holdings (especially the bigwigs), leading to a sudden sell-off.

But when people have invested their coins in the system, they won't just take off. They'll want to stick around and get back what they invested in the system.

See how that works?

Now, we'll be the first to admit that this system sounds crazy. But it has its perks:

- It's energy-efficient because expensive mining rigs are not required.
- It's fairer than a PoS system, which has been designed to favour the rich, who may only stake their large funds and do nothing, not even needing to sacrifice anything. Burning coins give someone the necessary merit in the system.
- The burning of tokens keeps inflation at bay.

Now, there are weaknesses, as well:

- Many people view burning tokens as a complete waste of valuable assets, and they don't buy it.
- This is still a niche consensus mechanism, and many people are skeptical.

In which platforms is PoB being used?

- Counterparty (XCP) uses PoB to create scarcity by burning Bitcoin to create XCP tokens.
- Slimcoin (SLM) also uses this mechanism for continuous sustainable mining.
- Factom (FCT) secures business data by burning Factom tokens to access the network.

Now that you understand how blockchain technology works, let's explore the various types of blockchain even further.

Chapter 6

Types of Blockchain

When people first hear about blockchain, they typically think of popular cryptocurrencies such as Bitcoin and Ethereum.

You are likely one of those people. So were we, in the beginning, at least.

Then you hear that blockchain has applications beyond cryptocurrencies in areas like healthcare, supply chain management, and government services, and you get confused.

How is it possible to apply this technology in such ways? Don't areas like these deal with sensitive data that should be kept private?

And you would be right to have such concerns.

But that's because you didn't know the whole story. And it's time we gave it to you.

You see, in reality, there are different types of blockchain aside from the one running Bitcoin.

They all have different features that make them suitable for the areas in which they are applied.

Let's look into them real quick, this time with finer details.

1. Public Blockchain

We'll start with the most common type you know about – public blockchain.

This type of blockchain is open and fully decentralised.

That's to say, anyone worldwide can join the network and start participating.

Also, there is no central party that governs or controls the network. The power rests in the nodes of the network.

Because the ledger is maintained by all the nodes in the network, there needs to be a way to verify the authenticity of the data contained inside.

That's where consensus mechanisms such as Proof of Work, Proof of Stake, Distributed Proof of Stake, and others come into play. They help the nodes verify the information, and if it's authentic, the block gets published.

Other key characteristics of public blockchains include:

- **They are transparent**: Everyone can see transaction data, so everyone knows.
- **They support many applications:** DApps, smart contracts, and NFTs. They are all run on public blockchains.
- **They promote interoperability**: Applications running on a public blockchain can easily communicate with each other and share data.

All these features sound cool, but public blockchains have their shortcomings, too:

- **Due to decentralisation and openness, you can't**

store sensitive information on them. Imagine a system storing business secrets or personally identifiable information. You can't keep that kind of thing public.

- **Transactions can be super slow for real-world use:** Think of it as seven TPS (Transactions Per Second) for Bitcoin and only fifteen TPS for Ethereum. That's crazy.
- **Scaling them is a nightmare**: How practical do you think it would be to scale Bitcoin's blockchain, for example?

Nevertheless, public blockchains are incredibly useful. They have wide applications in areas such as:

- Trading digital assets
- Crowdfunding
- Collecting donations
- Collaboration on open-source projects
- Creating tokenised assets
- ...And more.

Well-known examples of public blockchains are:

- Cryptocurrencies like **Bitcoin, Ethereum, and Solana.**
- **Decentralised finance (DeFi)** platforms such as Uniswap and Vaee allow for peer–to–peer lending without banks.
- **NFTs and Digital Art platforms** like OpenSea and Rarible enable artists to create and sell unique pieces.

2. Private Blockchains

Imagine you are the CEO of a significant industry heavyweight.

And you've heard that Blockchain is the next-generation technology in information management systems.

Relational Databases did well over the years but are dying slowly and will soon leave.

As someone who likes to be on the cutting edge of progress, you decide to investigate the matter and how you can become one of the early adopters of this revolutionary technology.

You start by asking yourself: What information are we keeping track of?

You come up with a list:

- Payroll
- Customers
- Suppliers
- Employee data
- Finances
- Market research

The list is long.

And that's when it hits you.

All this information is really private. It's crazy to imagine putting it out there in the public domain.

So, how is blockchain technology supposed to help you?

You'll ask yourself a question like that because you won't know that there's yet another type of blockchain you haven't considered – one that will certainly meet your needs.

A private blockchain.

As the name suggests, a private blockchain is one where access is restricted.

In other words, only authorised members can join it, read what's on it, or modify it.

Some key characteristics of private blockchains include:

- Usually, private blockchains are run by single organisations because they seek privacy, security, and efficiency.
- They are centralised, meaning the organisation that runs them has complete control.
- They are helpful when you seek to carry out precise organisational functions.
- They are faster because there are fewer participants in the network.
- They rely on a **Proof of Authority** consensus mechanism to maintain the data's integrity, plus adding new blocks.

What advantages can you expect from this type of blockchain?

- **It's faster and more scalable**, especially when compared to public blockchain. No matter your organisation's size, a private blockchain will meet all your needs.
- **It gives you more control and privacy**. And that is necessary in business. You can modify whatever you need to modify, and the public doesn't get a glimpse of inside information.

- **The energy consumption is low**. Definitely nothing compared to PoW public blockchain.

The main downside of private blockchains is that they are less decentralised, meaning that the entity controlling the network gets the most trust.

In a big organisation, this can lead to data manipulation and fraud.

So, what are some examples of real-world private blockchain?

- **Hyperledger Fabric** is a private blockchain developed by IBM, and it's used to manage supply chain information, so it's easy to track the source, reduce fraud, and improve efficiency.
- In Banking and Finance, JP Morgan uses **Quorum** to enable private transactions.
- In healthcare, **MediBloc** is often used to store patient records securely.

3: Consortium Blockchains

What does the word consortium mean?

The most standard definition is an association typically consisting of companies.

And that's really what the name **consortium blockchain** (also known as a **federated blockchain**) implies. It's a blockchain that a group of several organisation's control instead of just a single entity.

Because several organisation's control it, we might say that it is only partially decentralised.

In other words, it strikes a compromise between public and

private blockchains.

So, imagine several companies in a particular industry (like banking or health) decided to share critical information through a single tamper-proof database.

In that case, a consortium blockchain would make it easy to accomplish such a goal.

Suppose you recall our discussion on Proof of Authority. In that case, you already know how such a blockchain works and how its consensus mechanism operates.

Specific preselected nodes act as validators, ensuring all transactions are validated, and the blockchain is updated.

Now, because of the way consortium blockchains are structured, it's safe to say that they allow the members to share costs and risks.

What are some advantages of this type of blockchain?

- First, it's more decentralised than a private blockchain. That means no single entity exercises complete control over the network, lowering the risk of fraud and tampering.
- It is more scalable and efficient than a public blockchain.
- It's excellent for industries that need shared data.

But what about the downsides?

- The network can still be breached because it involves fewer nodes.
- It's less transparent when you compare it with a blockchain.

- It also creates a governance complexity issue. Organisations may not necessarily agree on rules and policies, making things difficult.

Despite these challenges, consortium blockchains are actively being used. For example:

- Ripple's blockchain **(RippleNet)** facilitates lightning-fast cross-border transactions among banks and financial institutions.
- **TradeLens**, which was developed by IBM and Maersk, helps companies track global shipments securely.
- The **MedRec blockchain** is allowing pharmaceutical companies to share clinical trial data securely.

And lastly, there's…

4: Hybrid Blockchains

The hybrid blockchain is the most interesting type on this list.

It works by combining public and private blockchain elements into a single structure.

So, an organisation can set up a public system that is permissionless on one side and private and permission-based on the other, sort of like a monster with two heads.

In so doing, the organisation can control the data, which users of that particular blockchain can access. Sensitive data can be stored privately, and non-sensitive data can be laid out for the rest of the world to interact freely.

So, what happens when someone wants to check sensitive data, perhaps to verify something crucial? The blockchain can allow them to do that via a smart contract.

Another thing to note is that hybrid blockchains are designed so that even the organisation owning the blockchain doesn't have the power to alter transactions.

Plus, when you join such a network, your identity remains secret, except when you engage in a transaction. In such a case, your identity is only revealed to the counterparty.

Alright, so given this unique design, what are the primary advantages of a hybrid blockchain?

- Because private information is stored in a closed ecosystem, the threat of a 51% attack on it is next to impossible.
- Scaling this type of blockchain is easier if you compare it to a public blockchain.
- Transactions are cheap and fast.
- Transparency can be customised depending on the person's view of what data is sensitive and should be kept secret.

Okay. And what about the advantages?

- We get tired of talking about this kind of blockchain, so developing it must be insanely complex.
- Some element of trust still needs to be bestowed upon the governing entity.

You now have a fairly good picture of what a hybrid blockchain is. Now, what is a good example of a hybrid blockchain?

- The **XinFin blockchain** that powers **XDC** enables financial transactions, allowing people to benefit from using a public ledger while still guaranteeing confidentiality in private transactions.

And that's it for the basics of blockchain. You are no longer in the dark about the internal workings of this revolutionary technology.

Moving on, we'll look at real-world applications of cryptocurrency and blockchain. See you in the next part.

Part 3:
Practical Applications

Chapter 7

Beyond Cryptocurrencies

Everyone knows how blockchain has led to the formation of cryptocurrencies.

But what are some other ways this remarkable technology is being put to use?

Here are a few that come to mind.

1. Identity Management

Identity management has always been the mainstay of big institutions like the government, banks, and corporations because they always need to verify people's identities.

But this type of management has always sucked for the following reasons:

- First, the information is generally stored in a centralised database. The problem with doing that is making the facility a prime target for hackers.

  For example, imagine what would happen if a hacker accessed the Equifax database. Think of all the personal data that is usually stored there.

  Oh, wait. It did.

In 2017, the Equifax database was hacked, and millions of Social Security Numbers were stolen. The company later spent a fortune compensating consumers who filed lawsuits.

- People have no control over what personal information companies collect and store in these databases. We don't know about you, but we'd like to understand what companies know about us.
- Traditional processes like visa applications or KYC (Know Your Customer) take forever. Who has that kind of time these days?
- Finally, people have learned how to use these systems to create fake identities and personal documents, which is why financial fraud and unauthorised access have become so common.

So, how is blockchain technology transforming this space?

- People will soon have control and ownership over their digital identities without relying on dubious third parties.

  For example, instead of IDs issued by the government being stored on central databases, people will now have the ability to store their credentials on a blockchain, granting access to various parties whenever necessary.

  The Sovrin Network is an example of a solution currently being developed for this very purpose.
- Digital identity solutions like **Microsoft's Identity Overlay Network (ION)** use blockchain to create tamper-proof records that governments and companies

can instantly verify.

Therefore, repeated verification methods that take up too much time will be unnecessary.

- **KYC** costs banks and other financial institutions billions of dollars every year as they seek to prevent fraud.

  Blockchain technology promises a secure system that can store the required data and share it securely across all banks, removing the need for redundant checks.

  A good example of a system that has already done this is **IBM and Securekey's Verified.** It is a platform that is currently doing a fantastic job in Canada.

- Governments are currently exploring the possibility of creating blockchain-based national identity systems, which could potentially be more secure and less bureaucratic, especially regarding matters like **passport/birth certificate** issuance or **voting** credentials.

  Estonia has already done this with an **e-Residency Program**. Their blockchain-based digital identity system allows global entrepreneurs to set up businesses remotely in the country.

However, identity management is only the tip of the iceberg. What about Governance?

2. Governance

Governments worldwide use databases to keep records, vote, make decisions, and for many other reasons we can't think of.

Many times, they even use paperwork.

These systems have always been inefficient for the following reasons:

- **Transparency is a huge problem**. Getting to government records isn't always easy. There's always some reason they can't give you what you want on time. And when transparency is an issue, who's to say people won't manipulate records or engage in corruption?
- **There is rampant fraud and a lack of security**. Think of how people have little faith in traditional voting systems. Plus, other less secure public records systems are vulnerable to hacking, tampering, and identity fraud.
- Paper-based systems, such as those for land registries and permits, are bloated with **bureaucracy** and **inefficiency**.
- Then there's the issue of **trust**. People in government institutions often can't be trusted. We've come to expect corruption, lack of accountability, and opaque decision-making from these people.

So, how can we expect blockchain to help make things better?

- Blockchain-based voting systems promise transparency and security. Every vote is recorded on the blockchain and can't be altered. Therefore, election results become trustworthy.

  A good example of such a system is **Voatz**. This system, which is based on blockchain, has been used for remote voting for U.S. citizens who are in the military or abroad.

Even countries like Sierra Leone used a blockchain-based system to count and verify elections in 2018 to prevent fraud.

- Blockchain promises permanent and transparent systems for recording transactions and ownership in public records such as property ownership, business licenses, and birth certificates.

  For example, Sweden has a land registry system called **Lantmateriet,** which uses blockchain, as we've just described, to curb fraud.

- And what about services like welfare programs, tax collection, and legal agreements?

  When it comes to that, governments are exploring using smart contracts to automate things, reduce human intervention, and promote efficiency.

  Dubai already has such an initiative for public services, aiming to be a blockchain-powered city by 2030.

- Regarding government spending, blockchain systems allow people to track activities in real time, ensuring that funds are being spent as intended.

  Citizens and watchdog groups can watch the government like a hawk and hold it accountable. The result is reduced cases of embezzlement and fraud.

  Ukraine is already using such a system.

3. Finance

The global financial system has traditionally been centralised by institutions like banks, clearing houses, payment processors, et cetera.

And while we have always relied on this system for global trade, it has also been failing us in the following ways:

- The process is insanely slow when you want to carry out cross-border transactions. That's because the process often involves multiple intermediaries, and it takes time to ensure that the books are correctly balanced so there are no discrepancies.
- Moving money across borders is also expensive. As we've already pointed out, multiple intermediaries are always involved, and each usually wants a cut of the money being moved.
- Traditional financial systems often come under attack because criminals stand to earn a big payday if they succeed.

  And criminals are creative. Banks may have strong defences guarding the money, but their customers and clients are often not savvy. So, schemes like identity theft and scams are much easier to pull off.
- Lastly, countless people worldwide are too poor to afford banking costs or don't have access to infrastructure. The vast majority of these people remain **unbanked**.

Blockchain technology comes to the rescue in the financial market in the following ways:

- The first application has to do with the removal of intermediaries. Blockchain allows people to transact any amount of money across borders instantly and cheaply. That kind of convenience is revolutionary.

  For example, instead of sending $10,000 and waiting days for the transaction to settle, a platform like Ripple (XRP) allows banks like Standard Chartered and Santander to facilitate instant transactions at low fees.

  Stellar (XLM) is another platform allowing the unbanked market in developing countries to access cheap financial services.

- **Decentralised Finance (DeFi)** is an emerging area of finance that uses blockchain technology to create **smart contracts** that replace traditional banking services like borrowing, lending, trading, yield farming, et cetera.

  And the cool part is that there are no intermediaries in DeFi. It's about people dealing amongst themselves.

  Isn't that beautiful?

  For example, places like **Aave** and **Compound** are basically DeFi platforms allowing users to borrow crypto-based assets without involving banks.

  Then, platforms like **Uniswap** and **Curve**, basically DeFi exchanges, allow for peer-to-peer trading. No centralised parties are needed.

- Did we also mention that blockchain allows people to tokenise real-world assets like real estate, stocks, art, et cetera?

By doing that, people can make these assets more liquid, divisible, and accessible to investors worldwide.

For example, a platform like **Securitize** is blockchain-based and does this. That is, it issues tokens that are backed by real-world assets.

Another good example is **RealT**, which uses blockchain technology to allow people to invest in fractional pieces of real estate.

- As for long-standing problems like identity fraud, money laundering, and data breaches, which have plagued this industry for ages, blockchain technology guarantees systems that offer tamper-proof digital identities.

  Such systems are a relief to financial institutions and a step up in security and compliance with regulations like **KYC (Know Your Customer)** and **AML (Anti-Money Laundering)**.

  A good example is a service like **Civic**, which aims to curb identity theft by providing a decentralised identity verification platform for companies in the financial sector.

  TrustChain, which was developed by IBM, is another blockchain-based platform that helps track high-value assets like gold or diamonds to prevent fraud in transactions.

- Then there are **CBDCs**. The acronym stands for **Central Bank Digital Currencies**. Many people believe that they are the future of fiat currencies.

They are similar to cryptocurrencies, except they are issued and controlled by the central banks of their respective countries.

The way we see them, CBDCs are a way for governments to keep up with the reality of digital currencies without giving up privileges like control and taxation.

Governments tout CBDCs as a financial innovation promoting inclusion, efficiency, and security.

However, many critics see CBDCs as a considerable threat.

CBDCs are programmable money.

Before you get excited about that, understand that the problem with government-controlled digital currencies is that the government can enact policies controlling how people use their money.

Think of how easy it would be for a government to cap how much money you can spend or what you can buy. And freezing your assets, for whatever reason, will be as easy as merely pushing a button.

No one should feel comfortable with such scenarios. They allow for the ultimate form of dictatorship by governments.

By that logic alone, cash is, in fact, a much more attractive proposition.

That said, whether CBDCs will eventually be adopted remains to be seen. We have a long way to go.

But that's not the case with countries like China. They have already adopted **Digital Yuan (e-CNY)**, and they report that it is a much more efficient system.

Also, as of this writing, the European Central Bank is exploring a Digital Euro project, which will be based on blockchain and allow for cross-border payments.

4. Healthcare

What about healthcare?

The health industry also deals with information systems that store large amounts of data.

But these systems have always been efficient for the following reasons:

- Doctors often have a hard time putting two and two together regarding patients' medical histories to get the bigger picture, mainly because their data is usually fragmented and scattered across various hospitals, clinics, systems… you name it.
- The information usually contained in healthcare records is often very sensitive and personal. For these reasons, this data is usually a prime target for hackers as it can have tremendous value.
- Different hospitals and healthcare systems typically adopt unique data systems, making the interoperability issue a genuine problem. In other words, sharing and accessing data across various systems is very difficult.
- Then you also have the issue of fraudsters who make false claims. Add to that problem, people who

routinely make billing mistakes, and you are looking at billions of dollars lost each year from the healthcare system.

So, how is blockchain technology helping address these issues? Let's look at some applications:

- First, blockchain makes it possible to have a tamper-proof single medical database for all patients. This database follows patients wherever they go.

  So, doctors and other healthcare providers can access real-time, up-to-date information on every patient.

  This option sure beats the idea of having multiple disconnected databases.

  A good example of a system like this is **MedRec**, from MIT Media Lab. It is built on blockchain, allowing patients to control access to who gets their information while ensuring data integrity simultaneously.

  Medibloc also offers similar functions.

- What would you do if you suddenly realised that the medication you take is fake?

  A good example is from the show *Archer* when Sterling receives terrible news from Krieger that he's been taking fake chemotherapy drugs.

  The reason why that's possible is blockchain.

  Systems such as IBM's **PharmaTrust** are powered by blockchain, allowing people to track the movement of pharmaceuticals across the supply chain and ensuring drugs are safe.

VeChain is another similar system used in China to track vaccines and medical supplies.

- And when it comes to patient records, years of watching shows like *The Blacklist* proved beyond doubt just how important medical information can be.

  In the wrong hands, it could be used for all kinds of criminal activities, including extortion.

  Fortunately, blockchain helps a lot in data security and privacy.

  By providing end-to-end encryption, blockchain technology ensures that only authorised personnel can access patient information.

  Patients can, in fact, grant and revoke access at will. That's a huge step up in security and privacy.

  BurstIQ is an example of a blockchain-based health data management platform that handles things as we've talked about.

  Another one is **Nebula Genomics**, a system that securely stores genomic data and allows people to have control over their DNA information.

- Then, you have the issue of claims processing in the insurance industry. People often complain of fraud in the industry, from both insurers and the insured. Also, unnecessary delays are part of the equation.

  Blockchain systems can automate verifications and reduce the chances of fraudulent practices.

  Also, smart contracts make it possible to have fast,

automatic payouts if specific conditions are met.

B3i (Blockchain Insurance Industry Initiative) is a consortium of major insurance companies using blockchain technology to ensure faster, more transparent claims management.

5. Supply Chain Management

Supply chains usually involve multiple stakeholders, such as manufacturers, suppliers, logistics providers, retailers, and consumers.

When there are those many people involved, tracking the movement of goods becomes urgent.

But doing so has always faced several problems because:

- Companies often use centralised databases to handle this kind of thing. Getting them to share information reliably is a headache, making it difficult to confirm product origins, manufacturing processes, and handling.
- Fake products can infiltrate supply chains, diluting the value of goods in areas like luxury, pharmaceuticals, and electronics.
- Many supply chains still heavily rely on paperwork to do their record-keeping. It's no wonder people have to grapple with huge delays and costs.
- When goods are defective, contaminated, or damaged, tracking them to do recalls, refunds, and solve other problems becomes a big nightmare for everyone and increases risks.

But blockchain is transforming the supply chain space in the following ways:

- First, blockchain promotes transparency in supply chains. Because everything about how a product is handled is recorded in an immutable ledger, it is easy for companies and consumers to check a product's origins, authenticity, and handling history.

  This kind of transparency can do wonders for some industries.

  For example, a product by **IBM** called **Food Trust** is being used by IBM, Walmart, Nestlé, and Carrefour to track products from farm to shelf.

  Doing so helps prevent food contamination and safety.

- Second, proving that a product is authentic and eliminating doubts that it's a fake will no longer be a problem.

  Blockchain helps provide digital certificates for products as well as tamper-proof records.

  Using a QR code scanner to verify a product's origin and handling through a blockchain record will be easy.

  And this is actually happening already.

  Services like **Everledger** are being used to track high-value items such as diamonds, vintage wines, and artwork to prevent the risk of counterfeits and fraud.

  VeChain is used for the same purpose by brands like Givenchy and Pfizer.

- Remember how we said paperwork is causing problems in supply chains? Think of all the contracts, custom forms, invoices, etc., that are usually involved.

Well, soon, that will be a thing of the past.

And it's all thanks to smart contracts.

Smart contracts enable the automation of various processes, reducing paperwork, processing times, and errors.

For example, **Tradelens**, which has been developed by IBM and Maersk, is a blockchain-based platform that digitises documents in the shipping business, reducing paperwork and delays in the industry by about 40%.

- As for defective or contaminated products, blockchain makes it easier for companies to identify and recall affected batches more efficiently, reducing risks and costs.

  As before, IBM's Food Trust is helping Walmart track contaminated foods in seconds instead of weeks. That helps prevent foodborne illnesses.

  Nestlé and Carrefour use blockchain to allow consumers to check product quality by scanning a QR code.

Now, as much as we've touched upon the various ways blockchain is being used in the real world, we must admit that the concept of smart contracts deserves more in-depth exploration.

In the next chapter, we'll be doing precisely that. See you there.

Chapter 8
Smart Contracts

You've heard a lot about smart contracts and their importance to the blockchain revolution.

But how well do you really know them?

If not much, this chapter will tell you all about them.

Let's start with what they are.

What Are Smart Contracts?

What are smart contracts in the first place?

The most common way to think about them is to imagine digital versions of traditional contracts.

Because that's what they really are.

However, the most official way to define a smart contract is a self-executing contract containing terms and conditions written in computer code format and that resides on a blockchain.

Is that clear enough?

With traditional contracts that we've always relied on, intermediaries such as banks, notaries, legal professionals, brokers, et cetera, have always been required to make things happen.

The problem is human involvement introduces all manner of errors and inconveniences.

Smart contracts compensate for traditional contracts' weaknesses by automatically executing when certain conditions are met.

That way, smart contracts make transactions faster, more secure, and more cost-effective.

What are the Key Features of Smart Contracts?

Smart contracts are distinctive and notable because they offer the following features:

- **Self-executing**: Essentially, this means that the code runs automatically by itself. There's no need for a human to intervene at all.
- **Immutable**: When a smart contract is deployed, no one can alter the code or interrupt its operation. It will execute exactly as intended.
- **Trustless**: Transactions are executed on the blockchain. Parties to a transaction need not trust each other or extend that trust to anyone. The system will ensure that the rules of the letter are followed.
- **Transparent**: The code for smart contracts is right there on the blockchain. Anyone can view it if they need to ensure it's legitimate.
- **Secure**: Because of the cryptographic and decentralised nature of blockchain, smart contracts are deemed to be highly secure and resistant to fraud, hacks, and manipulation.

Now you understand why smart contracts are so popular, how

about we look at how they work step-by-step.

How Smart Contracts Work

Step 1: Agreement Formation

Everything begins with two or more parties to a transaction defining the terms of engagement.

After they reach an agreement, the code is translated into a digital format that can be used on a blockchain. This code is the very essence of what a smart contract is all about.

To achieve this objective, a programmer must use languages specifically designed for writing smart contracts.

At the time of this writing, **Solidity** (for Ethereum) and **Ruby** (for Solana) are the most popular.

Step 2: Deployment on the Blockchain

Once the code has been written, it's time to deploy it on the blockchain platform so people can run it when needed, like uploading files to a server.

After the code reaches the blockchain network, it is assigned a unique contract address. If you know how IP addresses work in traditional networks, you know what we mean.

Once the assignment happens, the code will be available for use. It can be accessed and verified by all users of that particular network.

Step 3: Triggering Events

Now, the contract monitors the blockchain for events that match its conditions.

In traditional networks, this is similar to software services that listen on server ports for incoming requests from client computers.

And what events is the contract looking for?

We're talking about payments, delivery notifications, verification codes, and the like.

Once the proper conditions are met, the contract triggers the appropriate action. That might involve releasing funds, transferring ownership, or sending data.

Step 4: Automatic Execution

Lastly, the smart contract executes the transaction instantly and records the outcome on the blockchain for future reference.

The record remains permanent and tamper-proof.

Now that you've learned the basics of smart contracts, including how they work, let's dive into their significance.

The Significance of Smart Contracts

Smart contracts are changing the world.

Their ability to self-execute means they are revolutionising industries that have continuously operated with intermediaries.

The result is that inefficiencies are being reduced, costs are being brought down, and security is improving.

Finance, governance, supply chains, and real estate are improving.

Let's explore the details and their real-world impact.

1. Eliminates Middlemen and Reduces Costs

Third parties like banks, notaries, brokers, and lawyers have always existed in many processes.

Their roles have always involved handling matters like facilitating trust, ensuring legal compliance, providing access to markets, executing agreements, et cetera.

Because of their involvement, we often grapple with extra costs, delays, human errors, and corruption.

Smart contracts help remove those intermediaries, ensuring:

- Transactions take place directly between concerned parties, making things way cheaper.
- Legal and administrative fees either become lower or are removed entirely because they are enforced by code, not by professionals.
- Transparency increases as the contract logic is laid out for everyone to see, helping minimise disputes.

A good example of this is in real estate and property transfers.

Traditionally, buying a home has always been lengthy and exhaustive, involving all kinds of intermediaries such as agents, layers, escrow services, title companies, et cetera.

All these professionals charge fees, making transactions pretty expensive.

However, this will soon cease to be the case because smart contracts allow parties to exchange property directly and enforce the contractual details in code.

For example, a platform like **Propy** is a real estate blockchain platform that already allows people to transact properties without the help of real estate agents.

It is estimated that doing so cuts transaction fee by up to 30%.

Pretty cool.

In **Honduras**, the government is implementing a land registry system built on blockchain, and it is helping prevent land fraud and disputes over ownership.

2. Increases Efficiency and Speed

Up to now, regular contracts have always required:

- **Manual processing power**. For example, think of how long you have to wait for a mortgage application to go through.
- Crazy amounts of **paperwork** that need reviews, notarisation, and signatures.
- Unavoidable **delays** because of stipulated banking hours, human errors, and bureaucracy.

Smart contracts guarantee:

- **Speed of execution**: As soon as the right conditions are met, actions like payments and ownership transfers happen instantly.
- **24/7 Availability**: Blockchain networks are up practically all the time. You don't have to wait for operating hours to complete a transaction.
- **Cross-border transactions:** They can occur in minutes, compared to the days people are used to waiting in traditional banking.

To put this into context, consider the global trade finance industry. Its reliance on banks, customs agencies, and shipping companies results in long processing times and high fees.

The **Marco Polo network**, powered by **R3's Corda blockchain,** uses smart contracts to automate trade finance processes. As a result, payment times have been reduced from weeks to hours.

The same is true of the SWIFT systems banks have always relied on for international money transfers. Although they are super slow, they are now being replaced by Ripple's XRP ledger, which performs instant, low-cost international money transfers.

3. Improves Security and Trust

It is challenging to place complete faith and trust in traditional contracts for the following reasons:

- Anyone with enough motive, skill, or resources can forge documents. In fact, document forgery happens all the time. It's almost a joke.
- Documents can also be stolen or misplaced.
- Central databases can be hacked into, and personal or financial data can be stolen.
- Corrupt officials in places of power can alter records or ask for bribes in specific processes.

Thankfully, with smart contracts, you can put such concerns to rest because:

- Agreements are stored on blockchains, making them tamper-proof.
- There is no single point of failure in the network, which means that one of the nodes bearing the ledger can be removed or suffer a significant fault. Blockchain's decentralised nature ensures that the rest of the network can function as though nothing happened, making the smart contract service available 24/7.

- The network relies on cryptographic methods to secure transactions. That is as safe as anything can be.

How does all this apply in the real world?

Consider a case like the insurance industry. Fraud costs companies in this space billions annually because of false claims and manual verification errors.

However, a new trend is emerging: Companies like **AXA Insurance** use Ethereum contracts to enforce **flight delay compensation**.

In other words, if a delay occurs, the insured receives compensation immediately, eliminating the need for manual claims.

Another company that operates similarly is **Etherisc**, which provides decentralised crop insurance.

The interesting part is that the platform monitors real-time weather data and automatically pays farmers, preventing fraud.

4. Expands Decentralised Applications (DApps)

We'll talk about DApps in a later chapter, but for now, understand that they are applications that run on blockchain.

Some key characteristics of DApps are:

- Unlike traditional apps, which are run by the companies that developed them, DApps run without a central authority. For this reason alone, they are censorship-resistant.
- They are designed to operate transparently so that users don't have to place their trust in a particular company.

Smart contracts extend the functionality of DApps, making them even more powerful and valuable.

For example, here are key sectors that run DApps that have been powered by smart contracts:

- In **Decentralised Finance (DeFi)**, platforms like Uniswap, Aave, and MakerDAO run DApps that allow people to trade, lend, and borrow without involving banks.
- **NFT marketplaces** like OpenSea rely on smart contracts to allow people to buy and sell digital art without involving intermediaries.
- And platforms like **Voatz** use smart contracts to tally votes securely and prevent election fraud.
- Even blockchain-based games use smart contracts to handle player rewards, asset ownership, and in-game rewards.

  For example, **Axie Infinity** uses Ethereum smart contracts to allow players to own, trade, and monetise digital creatures.

Now, as cool as smart contracts sound, they are hardly the only hot game being talked about in town.

Non-fungible Tokens (or NFTs) are gaining momentum and buzz as well.

In the coming chapter, we'll examine NFTs and how they influence the creator economy. Stay tuned.

Chapter 9

NFTs and the Creator Economy

What are NFTs, and why should we care so much about them?

We'll start with a definition and get to the rest in a moment.

NFTs stand for Non-Fungible Tokens.

They refer to digital assets stored on a blockchain and represent ownership and authenticity of unique items.

That's an important statement to make because it makes a big difference.

For many years, creators, such as artists, musicians, and authors, have always grappled with the fact that someone can copy their work and claim it as their own.

Many techniques, such as copyrights, digital rights management (DRM), and watermarks, were invented to circumvent this issue.

Still, many people have been able to get around these schemes. Blockchain promises to introduce a new method that people can't easily defeat.

But before we talk about how that is possible, here's another question on your mind...

How are NFTs different from Cryptocurrencies?

We know it can be a little confusing. After all, they both reside on a blockchain.

The main difference is **fungibility**.

When we talk of fungibility, we refer to the property of a digital asset that allows it to be interchanged with other similar units.

For example, one bitcoin is fungible because it is identical to another and can be exchanged for it. The same goes for one US Dollar note. You can exchange it for another note because they represent the same value.

The same thing cannot be said for NFTs because they represent ownership of unique items.

Let's take art, for example. It is impossible to exchange the Mona Lisa for a painting done by Vincent van Gogh because they are both unique and don't have the same value.

Also, music done by Michael Jackson can't be traded in for a piece by Elvis Presley.

Does this make sense to you?

That **one-of-a-kind** nature is what constitutes non-fungibility.

Other key characteristics of NFTs that are worth keeping in mind and that distinguish them from other assets are:

- **Indivisibility:** Because each NFT has a distinct identity, it's impossible to divide it into smaller units the way you would divide something like a $100 note into five $20 bills.
- **They store ownership and authenticity data:** The records on the blockchain can accurately prove

beyond doubt who owns a particular NFT, making it impossible to forge.

- **Interoperability**: Today's NFTs are created for trading across multiple platforms and for use in various applications. This was not the case in the early days when NFTs were tied to the specific platforms on which they were issued.
- **Programmable**: NFTs also incorporate smart contracts, allowing cool features like royalty payments, unlockable content, and interactive utilities.

Okay, so now that you know how to differentiate NFTs from cryptocurrencies, do you ever wonder how they are created in the first place?

It's all through a process called Minting. Let's talk about that.

What is Minting, Now?

Minting is converting a digital asset (such as music, audio, video, or document) into a unique blockchain-based token that proves ownership and authenticity.

Once the minting process ends, the NFT can be stored on a blockchain. It can be readily sold, traded, or used in applications like gaming and the metaverse.

Here's how the process takes place step-by-step.

Step 1: Choosing a Blockchain

First, you must choose a blockchain that supports smart contracts.

In the beginning, this used to be **Ethereum**, but other platforms have joined in, such as:

- **Solana:** It is especially popular because it is cheaper and faster. Most gaming NFTs are minted here.
- **Polygon**: This one is related to Ethereum, except it charges a lower fee.
- **Binance Smart Chain** (**BSC**): This one is affordable and compatible with Ethereum tools.
- Others, like **Tezos**, **Flow**, and **Cardano**, are more eco-friendly and use proof-of-stake mechanisms.

Step 2: Selecting an NFT Marketplace or Minting Platform

The actual minting process requires a platform that supports the creation of NFTs.

At the time of this writing, some of the top options you have include:

- OpenSea: This one is the largest NFT marketplace, and with good reason because it supports Ethereum, Polygon, and Solana.
- Rarible
- Foundation
- Magic Eden
- Mintable
- Zora

Step 3: Setting up a Crypto Wallet

You'll need a crypto wallet to store the assets and pay transaction fee (gas fees in NFT terminology) to interact with NFT marketplaces.

Common wallets that people are using for NFTs include options like:

- **MetaMask**: This one supports Ethereum, Polygon, and Binance Smart Chain.
- **Phantom**: Supports Solana
- **Trust Wallet**: It supports multiple chains.

To put things into context, OpenSea users often plug MetaMask to mint and trade Ethereum-based NFTs.

Step 4: Uploading Digital Asset and Configuring NFT Metadata

Once you've connected a wallet to the minting platform, you need to upload your particular asset (image, music, gif, 3D model, et cetera) and start configuring the NFT metadata.

Metadata refers to attributes such as:

- **Name** and **description** of the NFT
- **Royalties**: How much will the creator make for every resale? (e.g. 10%)
- **Supply Type**: Is it Unique NFT (ERC-721) or Multi-edition (ERC-1155)
- **Unlockable content** refers to extra perks like exclusive files or membership access. For example, musicians like **Kings of Leon** always include bonus concert tickets in NFT purchases.

Step 5: Paying Gas Fees and Minting The NFT

Before the NFT can officially be added to the blockchain, it must be validated by paying gas fees.

Now, the cost of gas fees can vary depending on various factors like:

- **Congestion on the network**: The more users there are, the higher the fee will be. It's basic supply and demand at work.
- **Blockchain used**: Minting NFTs in Ethereum is way more expensive than options like Polygon and Solana.
- **Lazy minting**: Some platforms allow for lazy minting, creating NFTs without upfront costs and only charging fee when the asset is sold. OpenSea, for example, allows lazy minting.

Step 6: NFT is Minted and Listed for sale

After minting has taken place, the NFT is stored permanently on the blockchain, allowing for the following:

- The creator holding the asset as proof of ownership.
- Listing the NFT for sale on a marketplace at either a fixed price or for auction.
- Transferring or gifting the asset to another wallet.
- It can be used in games, metaverse worlds, or other token-gated communities.

So, now that you are familiar with how NFTs work, let's look at some real-world cases of this remarkable technology.

Use Cases of NFTS In Different Industries

NFTs are changing the world as we know it in the following ways:

1. NFTs in Art

The art world has always been remarkable for anyone fascinated by it. But it has always been plagued by challenges like the following:

- **No actual ownership**: This is especially true of digital art. It's way too easy to copy what someone else has worked hard to create and share it with everyone.

  Even in cases where someone's copy protects a creation, software tools are designed to break them. And that's just crazy.

- **Control by intermediaries**: Not everyone is into art. It's a niche market with very few participants, which has enabled intermediaries to thrive.

  If we wish to put up a painting for sale, for example, odds are 10 times out of 10, we would need to go through a broker.

  And brokers charge hefty fees, particularly in markets where liquidity is problematic. That's unthinkable, especially when brokers in any business make the most money, especially when considering the effort and resources expended.

  It's an ugly situation to find yourself in, and most artists wish things were different.

- **No royalties**: In most cases, when a piece of art gets sold, the artist loses its rights. So, for every sale that happens subsequently, they get nothing. It isn't kind, especially since many artists spend years honing their craft.

- **Forgery and authenticity issues**: You see it in movies all the time. Fakes are everywhere, and often, one must call an expert to judge the authenticity of a piece.

> It's always surprising how the difference between a real and a fake can be a single and simple detail. You often have to wonder how frequently experts get these details wrong and appraise an item as accurate when it's fake.

But thanks to NFTs, artists and participants in the art world will now get to enjoy conveniences like:

- **Proof of ownership and authenticity**: Because blockchain records keep track of every transaction with a particular NFT, you can be 100% certain that you are looking at the real thing and that someone is the real owner of a piece.
- **Direct access to markets**: Blockchain platforms like OpenSea and Foundation help artists resolve the middleman problem by bringing buyers and sellers to one place so they can transact fairly. It's a dream come true for most people in this space.
- **Built-in royalties**: The unfairness of artists no longer getting credit for their life's work is ending. Thanks to smart contracts that can be embedded in NFTs, the original creator can now be appreciated every time their piece changes hands.

Here are some examples of how NFTs are shaking up the art world.

- **Beeple** created an NFT artwork called ***Everydays: The First 5000 Days***, which sold for a whopping $69 million at Christie's.
- **Art Blocks** is using AI-generated algorithms to create one-of-a-kind art pieces that can be sold as NFTs.

- **The Doge NFT** was fractionalised, making it possible for thousands of people to own pieces of it – something never possible before.

2. NFTs in Music

Music is another thriving industry that has always operated inconveniently for the following reasons:

- **Overreliance on record labels**: As a musician, signing with a record label has always been necessary if you ever wished to have a career or even be taken seriously. And record labels are known for taking ridiculously massive cuts of artists' earnings.
- **Streaming services paying peanuts**: With platforms like Spotify and Apple Music, accessing a huge global audience must be cool.

  They listen, and you make big bucks with passive income.

  Tell that to any musician, and they'll laugh their buns off. They'll tell you that the best you can hope for with these services is a few cents per stream.

  And if you don't have a huge fan base, you might as well forget the whole idea.
- **Music piracy devalued work**: Hands up, if you haven't downloaded free music online.

  We can close our eyes and recall websites like *Mp3Skull.com*, which used to allow anyone to download virtually any soundtrack they pleased at zero cost.

  We even began to feel that we were entitled to free

music any time we wanted. It didn't matter to us that an artiste spent countless hours sweating at a studio and investing a fortune to create the piece we were enjoying for free.

It's been years, and while many piracy websites are long gone, new ones prop up every time, and the practice is far from over.

Plus, when people can't access them, they rip audio tracks from YouTube with online converters.

- **No control over secondary sales**: Let's say you try to sell an original copy of Michael Jackson's *Thriller* album today. How much money would go directly to the creator's family?

  If we had to guess, zero. Nada.

  And that's a big disgrace. The man was a total genius who worked like hell and staked everything he had at the time to make that album a reality.

NFTs will be a real blessing in the music industry because it's making the following possible:

- Musicians can mint songs as NFTs, sell them to their fans, and keep most of their profits.
- The same thing applies to fans who want premium experiences like concerts and content. NFTs allow musicians to sell such products without going through agents, who take huge cuts.
- Thanks to smart contracts, each time a music piece is resold, the artiste gets some credit through royalties.
- Fans can support artists directly on their projects, like being investors.

And this isn't all just theory.

Tory Lanez recently sold over a million copies of his *When It's Dark* album at $1 per piece, and it all happened in under an hour.

We're sure traditional labels wept when they heard that.

Snoop Dogg is following the same model, offering tracks as NFTs and giving fans limited access and rights.

We wouldn't be shocked to see other artists do the same thing.

3. NFTs in Gaming

What about the gaming world?

We've been involved in gaming for years and know the following to be true.

- In-game assets like skins, weapons, characters, et cetera, could be purchased, but they remained within the game's ecosystem, which is not interesting to most people.
- And even if in-game assets cost you money to acquire, there's nothing much you could do about them afterward. It's not like you could sell them to someone or transfer them in any way. It's no wonder people have never felt motivated to buy them in the first place.
- Let's say the developers of a particular game lost interest in it and decided to shut down the project. All the assets you accumulated through either effort or direct purchase would be lost. Forever. And that sucks!

But with NFTs being real, things have changed in this space. For example:

- It is possible to purchase the in-game assets we've discussed and keep them independent of the game.
- Some of these assets can be used across different blockchain platforms, even with games from other developers.
- You can keep and sell the assets for real money in secondary markets. Imagine that gaming assets being redeemable for cash. Wouldn't you love gaming just for that?
- With some games, you don't have to spend money buying assets. You can earn them by playing. That puts a whole new spin on the entire concept of gaming.

If all this sounds too idealistic to be true, **Axie Infinity** is a play-to-earn game that allows gamers to buy, breed, and later battle NFT creatures, earning cryptos in the process.

In **Sandbox** and **Decentraland**, you can enter a virtual world and buy NFT-based land, hold it, and later sell it, much like traditional investments work. You can also build experiences and sell other valuable items.

It's like playing GTA V and making actual money in the process. It's crazy.

In **Gods Unchained**, the same thing is possible. It's a card game that allows you, as a participant, to own NFT cards, which you can later sell for cash.

The trend has already begun, and we bet it won't stop soon.

4. Sports and Collectibles

And what about sports?

Indeed, this must be an obscure area where NFTs wouldn't apply in any way whatsoever.

Wrong.

Sports have always suffered problems like:

- **Traditional collectibles have always been physical**: Think about it. It's always been about trading cards, autographed jerseys, and memorabilia.

  Physical collectibles limit opportunities for many people who want in on the game.

- **Counterfeit collectibles**: Of course. Wherever there's money to be made, there will always be people looking to scam others and make off with some easy money. And so it is with sports collectibles. And when it comes to this, telling the real ones from the fakes is never easy.

- **Limited fan engagement**: What are the traditional ways fans have always shown support?

  It's the same as it's always been for a long time: buying merchandise, attending live games, watching broadcasts, that kind of thing.

  And that limits opportunities for many fans worldwide who want to contribute, particularly in this day and age of digital media.

- **Athletes have always had limited control over branding**: Traditionally, the industry has always left this part to sponsorships and licensing.

Thankfully, NFTs are here, and they are changing the sports industry in the following ways:

- **Sports collectibles can now be made digital:** Since they rely on NFT technology, their authenticity can be checked, so no holder can be duped. Their quantity can also be checked, so they remain rare and valuable.
- **Increased fan engagement**: NFTs can now be sold, allowing individuals to access exclusive experiences, VIP privileges, and ticketing.
- **Athlete empowerment:** A well-known athlete can monetise their influence by creating and selling their own NFTs in the open market. They no longer need to rely on a third party for this. Licensing and sponsorships aren't the only options available.

Are any of these options being used in the real world?

You bet.

For example:

- **NBA Top Shot** is a digital marketplace where fans can buy, sell, and trade officially licensed video highlights from the game as NFTs.
- **Sorare** is a fantasy soccer game where players can collect and trade NFT player cards.
- The **NFL**, **UFC**, and **MLB** are all considering launching their own NFTs collectibles and fan experiences.
- World-famous figures like **Christiano Ronaldo** and **Tom Brady** also release their NFT collections to connect with fans and build digital legacies.

5. NFTs in Real Estate and the Metaverse

And when it comes to real estate, anybody who's been involved in it knows that the following have always been true:

- **Transactions have always been slow and complex**. That's because, to buy or sell property, you have to consider multiple variables such as banks, agents, brokers, and legal paperwork, not to mention a lengthy approval process.

  Most people are impatient, and such considerations don't make them happy.
- **Deeds have always been stored in paper format and centralised databases**, and you know the trouble with such systems. Ownership records could be lost or tampered with, leading to fraud or unending disputes.
- **Large capital investment is required**. Real estate properties cost a fortune, meaning those who have invested in them have always been well-heeled individuals. And that makes for a tiny portion of the population.
- **Virtual Real Estate has always been a concept**. Yes, indeed, online worlds have always been around, but they haven't always had any monetary value.

But thanks to NFTs, we now have the following:

- **NFT property titles**: You can now represent property ownership as NFTs.

  Because of that, making transactions lightning-fast is possible while keeping them verifiable and secure.

  This is a development seasoned investors can term as magical.

- **Tokenised real estate**: Because real estate investments can be tokenised, fractional ownership of the underlying asset is also possible.

  In other words, investors can own real estate much like they would own a publicly traded stock.

  That makes it possible for ordinary investors who lack deep pockets to get involved in these markets.
- **Smart-contract-powered transactions**: Intermediaries who always have complicated transactions in the real estate (and also expensive) market can now be replaced with code that performs their functions in record time.
- **Metaverse land ownership**: Digital worlds allow people to acquire and develop virtual real estate based on NFTs with genuine economic value.

Is any of this fiction?

Heavens, no!

Consider the following:

- **Propy** is a blockchain-powered platform that allows investors to buy and sell real estate properties with NFTs.
- In places like **Decentralised** and **The SandBox**, the virtual real-estate game is already taking place, allowing people to buy, trade, and develop digital property.
- **Snoop Dogg** is one celebrity who has invested in virtual real estate. Word on the street is that he's already built a mansion, and fans are buying land around it.

- The **founder of TechCrunch**, **Michael Arrington,** recently sold a real-world apartment as an NFT via **Propy**.
- **Republic Realm** is a real estate firm that has already spent $4.3 million on metaverse land in **Sandbox**.

It all sounds good. We understand that the talk on the practical uses of crypto and blockchain technology isn't over until we touch on another crucial subject – **DApps**.

Meet us in the next chapter for that.

Chapter 10
Decentralised Applications

We've touched on decentralised applications (DApps) before. Still, we'll be the first to admit the conversation was slightly thin.

Let's deeply dive into them so you'll understand their role in today's digital landscape.

We'll start with the basics.

What in the World are DApps?

DApps are simply software applications that run on decentralised blockchain networks instead of centralised servers.

We realise that statement may sound like Latin, so let us explain.

Think of an app that's on your phone. Let's imagine the Facebook App, for example.

For you to use that app, the developers had to develop the source code for it, which allows you to communicate with friends and view content, which is the normal stuff you do on social media.

What you may not realise is that the core code for the Facebook app is stored on Facebook servers. Of course, the interface you interact with is also stored on your phone, but everything else happening behind the scenes is stored on Facebook servers.

You can pop up anywhere and log onto your Facebook account. The server can be reached remotely.

And that's how most apps work, really.

The thing with DApps is that they shift the paradigm from having a central server that stores the core code to having the code reside on a decentralised network of computers (the blockchain).

If you've used apps designed for torrent networks, you probably understand what we're talking about because the concept is similar.

The only difference is instead of referencing server source codes, torrent clients search for files stored on the hard drives of the networked nodes.

But that isn't all you have to know about DApps. Here are other key characteristics of DApps you need to know:

- The code is **open-source**. That means that the source code that makes the app run is open for the rest of the world to view and evaluate. This is a good thing because it allows for transparency.

  Closed-source software traditionally offered by companies hosting code on their servers can't be trusted. Sometimes, there are breaches of privacy issues associated with it.

- They are powered by smart contracts. We've discussed

smart contracts, so you know what they are and mean.

It also helps to know that conventional smart contracts form a key part of some DApps and influence how they function on the blockchain, especially regarding enforcing rules and logic automatically.

- Many DApps reward users and participants of the underlying blockchain with **tokens** for providing a crucial service to the network.
- **They are resistant to censorship**. Therefore, no central authority can take them down once they are functional.

Now that you know what DApps are and how they work, let's jump into real-world applications of this technology.

Practical Uses of DApps

Now, here's where things get a little confusing for many people.

When you look up practical uses of DApps on the internet, you often find that the applications overlap with those of smart contracts and NFTs.

For example, we saw earlier that smart contracts can be used to achieve **DeFi**.

Well, it so happens that **Decentralised Finance** is a key application of DApps, too.

The same thing goes for NFTs. We saw how games like **Axie Infinity** use NFTs. And **DApps** pretty much rely on NFTs as well.

So, what gives?

If you don't know much about computing and programming, it isn't easy to put two and two and figure out what may be going on.

Could it be that DApps are an entirely new area of Blockchain technology that is mysterious and independent?

No, not really.

The important thing is to understand that a DApp is the final deliverable that a blockchain technology consumer receives. Smart contracts and NFTs are merely components within that system.

Here's another way to look at all this:

- Smart contracts represent the **brains** behind DApps. They help the system to reason and arrive at logical decisions that benefit the user. Without smart contracts, a DApp wouldn't function.

  For example, **Uniswap** is a DApp that uses smart contracts to execute crypto trades automatically.

- As for NFTs, they represent the **ownership layer** of a DApp. This means they allow digital assets to be owned by the app users, making it possible for them to buy, sell, or trade.

  For example, Axie Infinity is a DApp that allows users to buy NFT creatures within the platform called Axies, which can be used in battle to earn rewards.

- Now, DApps represent the **functional layer** of the app, which brings everything together in one place with an interface that is convenient for the user.

Does all this make sense to you?

We feel compelled to talk about DApps as they apply to social media.

So, here we go:

DApps in Social Media and Content Platforms

We've been using social media platforms for decades now, and here are some ugly things we know about each one of them:

- **They own user data**. Facebook, for example, profits from user-generated content and sells user data to advertisers.
- **The control monetisation**. A platform like YouTube decides what creators earn, and they also set the rules as to what will and will not be allowed onto the platform.

  People who violate those rules risk getting kicked out of the platform entirely or being demonetised.
- **Free speech is limited**. The content on these platforms is highly censored. For example, many YouTube creators who have revealed content on gender issues, particularly those that shed critical light on women, tend to receive little or no exposure.

DApps are designed to remove corporate control in social media and give power back to the users.

For example, here are some things they guarantee:

- Users control their data, so no central authority can manipulate it or sell it to the highest bidder.
- Monetisation is made fair because the crypto is earned directly from users. No middlemen are involved.

- There is no censorship or blockage of accounts.
- Governance decisions are made by platform users, often through token-based voting.

Sounds almost perfect, but is any of this happening?

Yes. For example:

- **Steemit** is a blockchain-based blogging platform. Users who post blog posts there can earn STEEM tokens. There are no ads, just community-driven rewards.
- **Minds** is a social network that rewards crypto users for engagement, allowing free speech without corporate interference.

Now that you understand the real-world uses of blockchain technology, we'll dive into the risks this technology poses in the next part.

After all, we don't live in a perfect world, and even a brilliant technology like blockchain has weaknesses.

For now, we'll grab a cup of coffee.

Part 4: Cryptocurrency and Blockchain Challenges and Risks

Despite the remarkable power of blockchain and cryptocurrency technologies, they pose challenges and risks that we must be prepared to face.

The first step to handling their problems is to be aware of what they are. After that, it's possible to know how to address them.

Let's begin right away.

Chapter 11
Security Challenges

After all, we kept yapping in previous chapters about how crypto and blockchain were safe and virtually unhackable.

So, what's changing our minds?

We said that because blockchain technology tends to resist some well-known hacks of the past.

However, hackers are always innovative and tend to keep up with the times, like microorganisms. Sooner or later, they adapt, and new forms of hacks emerge.

Any computer security expert will tell you that no system is ever truly secure. While you can defend against known vulnerabilities, new flaws can be discovered in the future, which may compromise the system.

Plus, a human element in security tends to provide the weakest link, even when dealing with the most secure systems, and many people never know how to defend that front.

So, we will talk about the security challenges you will likely encounter with blockchain and crypto and how you may handle them.

1. Hacks

Hacks are the industry's most prevalent and often damaging security threat.

Here are some popular hacks that have wreaked havoc in recent times.

Exchange Hacks

This breach works because hackers target centralised exchanges where people hold cryptos in hot wallets.

Cryptos may be hard to break into, but hot wallets may not pose as much of a challenge to sophisticated hackers.

The goal is always to steal public and private keys stored in these wallets. Once that happens, the hacker can transfer the funds to their address of choice.

A good example of a famous hack of this type was **Mt. Gox**, the leading crypto exchange in 2014. Over $450 million was lost in bitcoins.

In another example, Coincheck was hacked similarly in 2018, and over $530 million in NEM tokens were stolen.

Prevention

So, what can you do to protect yourself from this attack?

- First, you can choose Decentralised Exchanges (DEX) instead of Centralised Exchanges (CEX). And if CEXs are the only option you can work with, find a reputable one that is likely to invest heavily in security.
- Second, you can opt to store your cryptos in a cold wallet. We already looked at how you can accomplish that in an earlier chapter.

DeFi Hacks and Exploits

DeFi platforms rely on smart contracts, which have vulnerabilities that can be exploited.

Some common exploits that hackers have used in the past with success include:

- **Reentrancy attacks**: This flaw allows hackers to repeatedly withdraw funds before the smart contract updates balance.
- **Flash loan attacks**: This is a technique where hackers use large, quick loans to manipulate prices and drain funds.
- **Oracle manipulation**: This is a scenario where hackers manipulate price feeds intending to distort values in smart contracts.

Examples of such hacks include:

- A 2022 hack targeted Axie Infinity blockchain bridge and led to the loss of $600 million.
- Also, in 2021, Poly Network was hacked, and $610 million were stolen. However, the hacker later returned the funds.

Prevention

How can you prevent such attacks?

Unfortunately, unless you are a programmer, this type of hack is difficult to defend against since it requires complex measures like:

- Performing rigorous smart contract code audits to ensure there are no flaws before launching any projects.
- Using multi-signature wallets for approvals.

2. Scams and Fraud

Remember how we said that the weakest link in secure systems is often humans?

Scams and fraud work like crazy because they exploit human gullibility.

Additionally, the crypto space lacks regulation and almost guarantees anonymity, which is a bad combination because it makes bad actors feel safe.

That said, watch out for the following:

Ponzi Schemes

This old trick is designed to fleece the public, where people are promised high returns.

It easily ropes people in because early investors are usually compensated with deposits from new investors, giving the impression that the promises of good returns are real.

Eventually, when the scheme cannot recruit new suckers, the fund collapses, and the original scheme creators make off with people's money.

This kind of thing happened with BitConnect, which lasted between 2017 and 2018.

It was a fictitious lending platform that promised people 1% daily returns. People lost over $2 billion when the scheme finally collapsed.

Prevention

The good news is that avoiding Ponzi schemes is easy.

Just watch out for financial opportunities with unrealistic returns and no transparent revenue model.

The best investments are straightforward, so do your research and find out how an opportunity is making its money.

If it's not as clear as the sky, run.

Phishing Attacks

Phishing attacks are also simple but remarkably effective for those who implement them.

A phishing attack occurs when a hacker clones a legitimate website that requires credentials, such as those for accessing a wallet.

Then he sends it to a victim and tries to trick them into using the fake link to sign in.

Upon signing in, the attacker harvests the credentials, which they can then use to steal money from the user's legitimate account.

Prevention

As formidable as phishing attacks sound, guarding against them is easy.

First, be wary of suspicious emails that ask you to give up credentials.

Also, always check the address bar at the top of your browser to confirm that you are working with a legitimate URL, not a fake one from a fake website.

This check alone pretty much thwarts all phishing attempts.

Rug Pulls

Rug pulls are like stealing candy from a baby's mouth.

The idea is for people to start a blockchain project—perhaps something related to an upcoming DeFi or NFT that they claim will change the world.

Then, they build hype around the project, eliciting excitement from the public and encouraging them to invest in it.

After they raise a large sum of money, they bolt, never to be heard from again.

And this isn't something we just dreamt up.

From 2014 to 2017, **OneCoin** was a fake crypto project in which a woman named Dr. Ruja managed to build a cult-like following worth $4 billion. The FBI is still looking for her after she mysteriously disappeared.

In 2021, another project called **Squid Game Token** lost investors roughly $3.3 million after its developers ran away with the cash, making it illiquid.

Prevention

The secret to avoiding rug pulls is to thoroughly investigate projects, especially new projects, before putting money into them.

Are the developers transparent and well-known?

Does the project create actual value?

And what are the liquidity lock periods?

If something looks dubious to you, avoid it.

Even better, stick with well-known crypto projects with a lot of credibility.

51% Attacks

This is a special type of attack where a malicious entity looks to gain more than 50% of a blockchain's mining power.

Once they do that, they gain control over the network, making it possible to reverse transactions, double-spend coins, and prevent new transactions.

They can even rewrite parts of the blockchain.

51% Attacks effectively hijack a blockchain network in cases where Proof of Work is the consensus mechanism used to approve new blocks of transactions.

51% Attacks have happened before in 2018 and 2020, Bitcoin Gold experienced this type of attack, and thousands of BTGs were double-spent.

In 2019, Ethereum Classic suffered a 51% attack, and $1.1 million was stolen in yet another double-spend.

So, yeah, this type of attack is pretty real.

But it's not likely to happen to Bitcoin and Ethereum.

And the reason why is simple.

Those two crypto coins run on the largest blockchain networks in the universe. Those networks have too many miners to beat, meaning such an operation would be absurd. It would require a boatload of money to set up, so hackers give up.

Prevention

Preventing 51% attacks is a matter of going with one of two choices:

- First, you can use an alternative consensus mechanism, such as Proof of Stake.
- Second, you can encourage the sign-up of several miners to the network so that the idea of overriding their power becomes outlandish and unfeasible.

But if you think security is the only challenge with blockchain, wait to hear how the government and its regulatory policies make things difficult for everyone.

See you in the next chapter for that.

Chapter 12

Regulatory Concerns and Government Policies

Dealing with governments and their policies is never easy in financial services.

However, knowing how to handle them is essential to thrive in the crypto and blockchain space.

Because, like it or not, governments make the rules, and its citizens had better follow them… or else.

So, what are the current concerns and challenges regarding the government and crypto?

Let's look at a few.

1. Varying Global Regulations – Different Approaches to Crypto

Governments around the world have taken different stances concerning the crypto issue.

We can divide the different stances into three:

- Pro-crypto nations
- Strictly regulated countries
- Crypto-banned nations

Pro-crypto Nations

These countries have adopted friendly regulations mainly because they believe in its potential for innovation.

Mostly, we're talking about countries like:

- **The United States of America**: Here, the government allows for crypto trading, but it still insists that strict regulations be enforced through the **SEC (Securities and Exchange Commission)** and **CFTC (Commodity Futures Trading Commission)**. Some crypto products are even classified as securities and must trade within the laws governing those securities.
- **Switzerland**: This country is famously known as "crypto valley" because it has clear regulations and encourages the formation of startups in the crypto space.
  The Swiss government even allows banks to offer crypto services.
- **El Salvador**: This country famously made news headlines worldwide when it accepted Bitcoin as its legal tender, allowing people to transact daily.
  It seemed like a risky option back then, but with Bitcoin prices sky-high today, many people feel it was the right move.

Strictly Regulated Countries

Then, you have countries that have accepted crypto but have decided to exercise strict regulations.

You might say the governments in these countries are pretty skeptical about the impact crypto might have on their economies, so they want to exercise as much control over it as possible.

We're talking about countries like:

- The **EU**, which has implemented **MiCA (Markets in Crypto Assets)** regulation, which standardises licensing requirements for exchanges and imposes strict **anti-money laundering (AML)** rules.
- **Japan** has allowed crypto trading but requires exchanges to be registered and follow **anti-money laundering** laws.
- **India** has permitted crypto, but taxation is at **30%** on capital gains and **1%** transaction tax.

Crypto-Banned Nations

Lastly, you have governments that have completely banned crypto and want nothing to do with it.

To them, crypto lays the groundwork for financial instability and illicit activities.

In this category are countries like:

- **China** banned crypto mining and trading in 2021, citing financial risks and money-laundering concerns. But the government ultimately favours its digital currency, the Digital Yuan.
- **Egypt, Morroco, and Algeria:** These countries have outlawed crypto as they see it as a significant financial risk.

2. Taxation

And when it comes to taxation, we've observed that most countries view crypto as taxable property rather than a currency.

They tax crypto, which is how they could tax any other security. For example, most countries impose two types of tax on crypto:

- **Capital gains tax**: In other words, buying something like Bitcoin today and having it increase in value. Once you sell it, the profit you accrue is called capital gains and is subject to taxation.
- **Income tax**: Let's say you engage in crypto mining activities or receive payments for goods or services rendered in crypto. That money is taxable at various rates.

Many countries impose crypto taxation, and if yours hasn't yet, it's best to assume that it's only a matter of time.

For that reason, here's what you can do to stay compliant:

- Keep accurate records of all your crypto transactions
- Use crypto tax software. Products like **CoinTracker** or **Koinly** are ideally suited for the job.
- Report all your gains and losses when tax filing season comes around.

Privacy Concerns

Most people who love crypto are thrilled about its potential to offer financial privacy.

However, many governments are pushing for **KYC (Know Your Customer)** and **AML (Anti-Money Laundering) laws**.

These types of regulations require crypto users to reveal their identities, and that's something that doesn't make a lot of people happy.

Also, governments now insist on **tracking wallets and transactions** so people don't cheat on their taxes.

Here are some examples of what we're talking about:

- In the U.S., FinCEN requires that all centralised crypto exchanges enforce KYC.
- In the EU, the MiCA regulations require that all providers of crypto wallets collect and share user data.
- India also enforces KYC for all crypto exchanges.

So, what can you do to maintain some semblance of privacy in a crypto world?

If privacy is essential to you, here's what we'd recommend:

- Use decentralised wallets like **MetaMask** or **Trust Wallet** instead of centralised exchanges to manage your money.
- Opt for privacy coins like **Monero** and **Zcash**. But keep in mind the legal risks.
- Use exchanges that enforce KYC and are also strong on user security. **Kraken** and **Binance** are known for this.

Potential Future Regulations

Regulations keep evolving, and we will likely see new ones.

For example, we advise you to keep a close eye on:

- **Stablecoins**: Many governments worry about the potential of stablecoins disrupting the financial markets. That's why some nations are considering CBDCs.

- **Crypto Taxation Laws:** We envision a scenario where automatic tax reporting on crypto transactions is the norm.
- **KYC on DeFi:** As DeFi becomes increasingly popular, governments will want to know what's happening there and who's participating.
- **NFT and Metaverse Regulation:** Governments will likely start tracking **NFT sales** and enforcing **content ownership rights** in the Metaverse.

How to Stay Compliant

Now that we've established that the government is very much involved in crypto, what must you do to stay on the right side of the law?

- Read often and stay updated on regulations governing crypto in your country.
- Use regulated exchanges that comply with local laws.
- Keep detailed records of your transactions for when the taxman comes knocking.
- Consult tax experts for advice on crypto-related tax issues.
- Be cautious about using privacy coins or DeFi platforms in highly regulated regions.

But regulations aren't the only difficulty you have to worry about. Market-related worries like price volatility are a big issue in this space.

Let's look at that in the next chapter.

Chapter 13

Volatility in Cryptocurrencies

Cryptocurrency prices move fast. One day, you're up 50%; the next, you're down 30%.

Some people think that's exciting. Other people think it's terrifying.

Personally, we think terrifying is the more accurate answer.

Instead of remaining fearful about a particular situation, we prefer to understand the issue and know how to deal with it.

And that's what we'd like to focus on in this chapter.

Why Crypto Prices Fluctuate

Unlike traditional markets, cryptocurrencies can experience wild price swings in a matter of hours.

Why does that happen? We can think of a few reasons to explain it.

1. Supply and Demand

Like any market, crypto prices are driven by **supply** and **demand forces.**

The limited supply of something like Bitcoin (capped at 21 million coins) creates scarcity.

Its price surges when many people want something, yet it's available in limited quantities. A bit like gold, we might say.

And demand for crypto has been rising for various factors, such as:

- **Mainstream adoption by major companies**. If people see the big boys buy, they'll want to buy, too.
- **Fear of missing out**. As prices rise, more and more people wish they were in the game, so they get in.
- **Institutional involvement**. When large investment companies and banks like JP Morgan and Goldman Sachs step onto the scene, that's a significant signal to the public.

Now, let's look at the opposite. What do you think happens when prices are sky-high and people suddenly get cold feet?

Panic selling follows, of course. And prices fall sharply.

2. Speculation and Hype

Another reason why prices gyrate like wild horses is because crypto is mostly a speculative market.

It is primarily influenced by gossip and emotions rather than fundamentals.

So, when someone influential like Elon Musk tweets, you can expect prices to react.

And when regulation news comes in, people will place a lot of importance on the issue, and prices will move significantly.

What about when a new coin comes on the market?

Because people think crypto will be the next big thing tomorrow. They have seen what has happened with Bitcoin and Ethereum. There will likely be a buying frenzy as people try to get in at the bottom.

3. Market Liquidity

Liquidity refers to how easily an asset can be bought or sold without affecting its price.

With traditional stocks like Tesla or Apple, prices are more stable because millions upon millions of buyers and sellers are in the market for it at any given time.

But that's not the case with crypto.

It's a niche market that has yet to receive wide public acceptance. This crazy market is mainly populated by geeks like you and me.

When traders are few, any significant development moves prices like crazy. For example, an investor with $100 million in a market like Apple stock may not see the price move even by an inch.

However, such an infusion of capital in something like Ethereum will cause a surge in price.

The same goes for selling. If some hedge fund decides to dump its Bitcoin holdings, we can guarantee that the particular action will cause the price to fall faster than a rock.

That's what low liquidity does to a market, and crypto is rife with it.

4. Regulatory Uncertainty

Governments are still figuring out how to regulate crypto, which creates uncertainty.

When people are uncertain, even a small development will make them act.

Let's say China suddenly declares crypto trading legal. We can almost guarantee that Bitcoin will surge when that news hits the wires.

But let's say the U.S. president comes out and says he will tighten the crypto grip, especially since it allows people to skirt sanctions.

Such a statement will likely cause the price to fall.

Again, it sounds crazy, but that herd mentality reflects how most speculative markets operate.

Until regulations are clear and consistent, the crypto markets will remain unpredictable.

Risk Management Strategies

So, what can you do to minimise the risk in your portfolio as a crypto investor?

Here are some ideas:

Do Your Research (DYOR)

Don't go with public sentiment. Just because Taylor Swift says something about crypto on Twitter doesn't mean you should rush to act.

That's a sure way to get burned in any financial market, not just crypto.

Instead, conduct thorough research and place your bets based on solid reasons that only you are confident in.

Diversify

This is another big one.

The truth is, no one knows what might happen tomorrow in

any market. And because you are not a fortune teller, it's just too damn risky to hold all your money in one place.

What if governments worldwide ban crypto, effectively sending prices to practically zero? You would lose everything.

The good news is that it's almost impossible for all markets worldwide to react the same way.

So, if you hold only a portion of your investment capital in crypto, you will not likely get wiped out, no matter what happens.

Set Stop-Loss Orders

This is an important advice, especially if you are trading in crypto.

Every time you place a bet in crypto, determine your automatic selling point if the idea you had in mind doesn't pan out.

That prevents you from losing all your money on a sour bet.

It may sound like a boring idea. After all, the market may come back after taking you out.

But suppose you operate with a sound methodology in the first place. In that case, it's almost impossible to go bankrupt **if you place a stop-loss order** on the market that limits your losses to just a tiny percentage of your capital, say 1%.

Invest What You Can Afford to Lose

Last, only invest money you can lose and still function like a normal human.

You must accept the reality that you might lose your entire capital. If that happens, what will happen to you?

If you can imagine your life going to hell, then it means you are taking too much of a risk.

When there's too much at stake in the markets, the chances are high that you'll lose your objectivity. When you lose that objectivity, you start to gamble and take on excessive risk.

And while taking on significant risks sounds like fun - after all, people say that significant risks come with big rewards - the reality is that substantial risks often come with a greater probability of getting wiped out.

It's often better to play it safe in the crypto markets. And if things go wrong, you can chalk it up to experience and call it a noble experiment.

This will allow you to approach it again if you have the chance or comfortably move on with your life.

Chapter 14
Future Perspectives

The Future of Cryptocurrencies

Let's take a trip into the future.

Close your eyes and picture this: You walk into your favourite coffee shop, order a cappuccino, and pay with Bitcoin.

There are no credit card fees and no bank delays. Just a quick tap on your phone, and you're done.

Later that afternoon, your paycheck arrives in Ethereum and is deposited directly into your digital wallet.

Then think of banks no longer being part of financial transactions: Loans, mortgages, and savings accounts—everything managed through **decentralised finance (DeFi)**, where smart contracts handle everything automatically.

Sounds like a movie.

Is this really the future we're heading toward?

Let's look at what's happening right now—and what the experts predict for the years ahead.

Predictions and Trends

Cryptocurrencies have already upended the financial world, but they're still evolving.

The next decade is likely to bring even more significant changes, such as:

1. More regulation.
2. Governments are no longer ignoring crypto.
3. From the U.S. to Europe to China, policymakers are stepping in to regulate the industry everywhere.

But if you think about it, regulation isn't necessarily bad news.

Here's what we mean:

- **More rules equal more legitimacy:** Big businesses feel more confident jumping in when governments provide clear regulations. That could lead to **greater adoption** of crypto worldwide.
- **The crackdown on fraud:** Rug pulls, pump-and-dump schemes and exchange collapses have given crypto a bad name. Stricter laws could help **weed out the bad actors** and build trust.

Despite all this, there's a downside.

Overregulation could stifle innovation or make crypto look more like traditional finance, defeating the whole purpose of decentralisation.

Expect a tug-of-war between innovation and control as governments try to rein in crypto without crushing it completely.

Institutional Adoption

Once upon a time, crypto was just a niche hobby for tech geeks and risk-tolerant investors.

But that's not the case anymore.

- Hedge funds, pension funds, and even major banks quietly buy **Bitcoin and Ethereum**. For example, a story by Yahoo Finance talks about how Goldman Sachs has loaded up with nearly $2 billion in Bitcoin and Ethereum
- BlackRock, the world's largest asset manager, has already **launched a Bitcoin ETF**.
- Companies like **Tesla and MicroStrategy** hold **billions of dollars** in Bitcoin.

What do all these developments mean?

Only two things:

- If big institutions continue buying in, crypto prices could skyrocket.
- Traditional finance and crypto may merge rather than compete.

The only question that doesn't seem to have a straight answer is whether crypto will still be a tool for earning financial freedom for the masses or just become another asset class controlled by Wall Street.

Only time will tell.

Mainstream Payments

Looking back to the coffee shop scenario we related earlier. Can we really expect crypto to replace credit cards?

Probably yes. But we don't think any of it will happen overnight. It'll be a slow and gradual process.

Here's what is currently happening:

- **Visa and Mastercard** are already integrating crypto payments.
- **PayPal and Square** allow users to buy and spend crypto.
- **El Salvador made Bitcoin legal tender**, so it's reasonable to expect that other countries may follow suit.

So why aren't crypto payments the norm yet?

There are good reasons why it hasn't happened yet:

- **Transaction fee and speed** – A currency like Bitcoin is still **too slow and expensive** for small purchases.

  The good news is that newer cryptocurrencies are built to compensate for that weakness.

- **Price volatility** – It's hard to imagine ordering a coffee for $3, but by the time the transaction clears, it's worth $5. No one wants to transact with something that behaves like that.

So, until these issues are solved, crypto will unlikely replace cash and credit cards. Still, it could become a common alternative—especially in unstable economies.

Central Bank Digital Currencies (CBDCs) – The Government's Answer to Crypto

Have you wondered what the governments worldwide are thinking when they look at crypto becoming increasingly popular worldwide and them doing nothing about it?

Well, they actually are.

Governments have examined the situation and decided they don't like the idea of losing control over money. How else will they be able to tax it? How will they maintain a competitive advantage over other economies? How will they not get sanctioned by the powerful nations?

So, instead of fighting crypto outright, they're creating their own digital currencies.

We've talked about them before. They are called **Central Bank Digital Currencies** (**CBDCs**).

Think of a **CBDC as a government-backed stablecoin**—a digital version of your country's currency controlled by the central bank.

And some parties are already leading the charge:

- **China** is ahead of the game with the **Digital Yuan**, which is already being tested in major cities.
- The **European Central Bank** is working on a **Digital Euro**.
- The **U.S. Federal Reserve** is exploring a **Digital Dollar**.

- The **RBI India** is exploring **Digital Rupee.**

CBDCs are likely to lead to benefits such as:

- **Faster payments** – No more waiting days for bank transfers to clear.
- **Financial inclusion** – People without bank accounts could access money digitally.

It all sounds good, but there's another side to CBDCs:

- **Total government control:** Unlike what we've seen with crypto, CBDCs are **not decentralised**. They are controlled by a single entity – the government.

  That means the agencies could track every transaction or even freeze accounts at will.

- **The death of cash:** If CBDCs replace physical money, it could lead to a world where every transaction is monitored.

  What could that mean when dictators get a hold of this technology?

  Things could get murky quickly.

CBDCs vs. Cryptocurrencies

Another question to ask yourself is:

Will CBDCs **coexist with crypto**, or will they **compete**?

Mmm. Interesting question.

We're not psychic, so we don't have the answer, but we can imagine some scenarios:

Scenario 1: They Work Together

The first possibility is that CBDCs could be used for everyday transactions. At the same time, Bitcoin and Ethereum remain **alternative assets** like gold.

Scenario 2: Governments Try to Rail Guard Crypto

The second scenario is that some countries may **restrict decentralised cryptocurrencies** in favour of government-controlled CBDCs.

No one knows which scenario will win. But one thing is sure: The battle between **decentralisation and control** is just beginning.

Blockchain Evolution

If you imagine crypto being a car, blockchain is like the road it drives on.

And from the look of things, that road is about to get a serious upgrade.

Look at it this way: the early days of blockchain were like the first generation of the internet.

For those who existed then, you can remember that it was slow, clunky, and limited.

Same deal with crypto.

In the beginning, something like sending Bitcoin took forever, Ethereum gas fees could cost more than your transaction, and different blockchains operated in silos, unable to communicate with each other.

But change is coming. And fast.

Let's explore what's next for blockchain technology and why the future looks exciting—and a little scary.

Emerging Technologies

Layer 2 Solutions: Fixing the Speed and Cost Problem

You decided to send Bitcoin or Ethereum during a market frenzy. What do you think would happen?

We'll tell you: It'll possibly take hours—and cost a small fortune in fees.

Why?

Because Bitcoin and Ethereum, the most prominent blockchains, operate like congested highways during rush hour.

The more people use them, the slower and more expensive transactions become.

That's why **Layer 2 solutions** are considered a game-changer.

Layer 2s are like express lanes on a freeway. They take transactions **off the main blockchain**, process them **faster and cheaper**, and then send them back to the leading network to be recorded securely.

Bitcoin's **Lightning Network** is the most famous layer 2 blockchain scaling example.

Here's what it does:

- It allows people to make instant Bitcoin payments with near-zero fees.

- It happens in milliseconds instead of waiting ten minutes or more for a transaction to confirm.
- People are already buying coffee with Bitcoin in El Salvador using Lightning.

Ethereum has its own Layer 2 solutions, like **Arbitrum, Optimism, and Polygon**, which drastically reduce gas fees and increase speed.

What does this mean for the future?

- **Crypto payments could become mainstream.** No more insane transaction fees for a simple purchase.
- **NFTs and DeFi platforms will be more accessible.** No one wants to pay $50 in fees to buy a $10 NFT.

Layer 2 solutions are turning blockchain from a traffic jam into a fast, efficient highway—and that changes everything.

Cross-Chain Interoperability

Right now, most blockchains don't talk to each other.

Bitcoin, Ethereum, Solana, and Cardano operate like isolated islands in the ocean. If you want to move assets between them, it's a nightmare.

Imagine if every bank in the world operated on a different system, and you had to go through a complicated process to transfer money between them. That's the current state of blockchain.

Cross-chain interoperability aims to fix that by creating a universal translator for blockchains.

So, instead of needing separate wallets and different bridges to move assets, cross-chain technology will allow seamless transactions between different blockchains.

Some major players in the space include:

- **Polkadot & Cosmos** are explicitly built to connect other blockchains and enable smooth communication.
- **Wrapped tokens (like Wrapped Bitcoin on Ethereum)** are a temporary fix that lets you use Bitcoin on Ethereum-based platforms.
- **Chainlink's Cross-Chain Interoperability Protocol (CCIP)** is a work-in-progress solution that could create true cross-chain functionality.

Why should you care too much about interoperability?

Let's look at a few scenarios that highlight the importance:

- Imagine instantly trading assets from Ethereum to Solana without relying on a centralised exchange. Wouldn't that be lovely?
- Also, DeFi platforms could become truly decentralised, no longer confined to one blockchain.
- Game developers could create NFTs that work across multiple ecosystems.

With interoperability, we're moving toward a blockchain ecosystem where everything is connected. And that's a pretty big deal.

Quantum Computing

If you've been paying attention to the latest developments in the tech world, chances are you've heard about quantum computing.

But what relationship does it have with blockchain?

Let's look at it from a security perspective.

Blockchains are incredibly secure because of cryptographic encryption. Hacking Bitcoin's encryption with current computers would take thousands of years.

But what happens when computers get millions of times more powerful?

That's where quantum computers could change the game completely.

Quantum computers can perform complex calculations in seconds, which would take today's computers centuries to complete.

So imagine what they would do if the wrong people started using them.

Here are some things that could happen:

- A powerful enough quantum computer could theoretically break Bitcoin's encryption in minutes.
- And that computer could also hack wallets, forge transactions, and unravel blockchain security.

Scary stuff.

Does this mean crypto is doomed? Not necessarily.

Experts are already working on **quantum-resistant cryptography**, which could immune blockchains to quantum attacks.

There are two possible futures here:

- There's what we would call a **Doomsday Scenario**. In this scenario, quantum computers break blockchain security before we have a solution. Chaos ensues, and Bitcoin and Ethereum become worthless overnight.
- Then, there's also a **survival scenario** in which blockchains upgrade to **quantum-proof encryption** before quantum computers present a real threat. Crisis averted.

Some projects, like **QANplatform**, are already building quantum-resistant blockchains.

So, should you panic?

Not yet. Quantum computing is still years (if not decades) away from being a real threat.

But it's something the blockchain world can't ignore.

Ethical and Environmental Considerations

If you remember the old Spiderman movie, you know the phrase: "With great power comes great responsibility."

Well, it's kind of true, especially in the crypto world.

Crypto is shaking up finance, decentralising power, and giving people control over their money like never before.

But with that disruption comes controversy. Critics claim it's wrecking the environment, enabling fraud, and creating an unregulated Wild West of finance.

Is that fair?

Let's examine blockchain's ethical and environmental dilemmas—the real issues, the misconceptions, and the solutions that could reshape crypto's future.

Blockchain and Sustainability: Is Crypto Killing the Planet?

Think of headlines like these:

- *Bitcoin mining consumes more energy than entire countries!*
- *Blockchain is an environmental disaster!*

It sounds like the world's end, but is that the whole story?

Not exactly.

Let's see why.

Proof of Work vs. Proof of Stake

As we saw earlier in this book, Bitcoin's energy-guzzling reputation comes from **Proof of Work (PoW),** the consensus mechanism Bitcoin and early blockchains use to verify transactions.

Miners compete to solve complex puzzles to validate transactions and secure the network.

And that takes massive amounts of electricity because they make computers run mad.

For example, Bitcoin alone consumes around **120 terawatt-hours of energy per year,** which is comparable to the entire country of Argentina.

But the situation isn't as grim as it sounds for a few reasons.

- The first is that mining is shifting toward renewable energy. Many mining farms now operate on solar, wind, or hydroelectric power.
- Second, PoW is being replaced. Ethereum, the second-largest blockchain, ditched PoW and moved to Proof of Stake (PoS) in 2022, reducing its energy consumption by **over 99% overnight.**

And that's not all.

Green Blockchains

The blockchain industry is actively working on sustainability solutions.

Some new blockchains are designed to be eco-friendly from the start:

- **Cardano** and **Solana** use PoS, which consumes minimal energy.
- **Algorand** is **carbon-negative**, meaning it actively offsets more carbon than it produces.
- **Chia** claims to be a **"green blockchain"** using a controversial consensus mechanism called proof-of-space instead of energy-intensive mining.

So, is crypto terrible for the environment? There is an energy problem, but solutions are already here.

We could see a carbon-neutral or even carbon-positive blockchain world in the future.

The Ethical Side of Crypto

Crypto is revolutionising finance, but like any powerful tool, it can be used for good and bad.

Let's talk about the dark side.

1. Scams & Fraud

Crypto is the ultimate financial freedom tool—but with no central authority, bad actors thrive.

Some threats we've discussed before include:

- **Rug pulls:** Where developers create a flashy new token, hype it up, and then disappear with investors' money.
- **Pump-and-dump:** Influencers artificially increase a coin's value, cash out, and leave retail investors holding worthless tokens.
- **Hacks and exploits:** DeFi platforms lose **billions of dollars** each year due to hackers taking advantage of weak security.

Crypto's lack of regulation makes it a paradise for scammers—and until security improves, this will remain a significant ethical issue.

2. Privacy: Who's Watching?

One of crypto's most significant promises is financial freedom—but is it leading us toward total surveillance?

It's not such a simple question.

There are two sides to this coin.

On one side, cryptocurrency allows people in authoritarian regimes to escape financial censorship.

For example, privacy coins like **Monero** protect users from government overreach.

But then there's another side where governments are pushing to adopt **CBDCs (Central Bank Digital Currencies)**, which could track every transaction you make.

Also, some governments want all crypto transactions to be traceable.

If governments eventually have their way (and we think they might), you can say goodbye to financial privacy.

So, where does that leave us? What's the future?

If we had to guess, striking a balance between security and privacy would be one of the most significant ethical battles in the crypto world.

Adoption and Inclusion

Contrary to many people, blockchain isn't just about making millionaires.

We've seen stories of early Bitcoin investors turning pocket change into fortunes. But the real benefit to the rest of the world isn't wealth creation but financial empowerment for the billions of us who lead everyday lives.

For example, thanks to blockchain:

- A farmer in Kenya can receive payments instantly from anywhere in the world without relying on a corrupt and greedy banking system.
- A small business in India can access loans through DeFi, skipping the red tape of traditional banks.
- A refugee fleeing war still has access to their savings, even if they've lost everything else.

These are all benefits that we could use more of.

Let's look deeper into this issue.

Empowering Underserved Communities

It's known that roughly **1.4 billion people** worldwide have no bank account access.

That means no loans, credit, secure savings, et cetera; people are just living like the Stone Age.

And that's just not okay.

Blockchain can change that by offering borderless, decentralised financial services that don't require a bank.

For instance:

- With just a phone and an internet connection, anyone can send and receive money instantly, skipping the slow, expensive process of traditional banking.

- If someone has no credit history, banks won't even look at that person twice. But blockchain says, "No problem." **DeFi** platforms let people borrow, lend, and earn interest without a bank's approval.
- People can't prove ownership of their land, money, or identity in many parts of the world. However, **blockchain-based digital IDs** could change that, giving people control over their assets.

And it's already happening, by the way:

- In **Nigeria, Kenya,** and **El Salvador**, people have used **Bitcoin and stablecoins** to escape unstable local currencies.
- In **Venezuela**, families rely on crypto to survive hyperinflation.
- In **Afghanistan**, women have used Bitcoin to maintain financial independence in the face of oppression.

Blockchain offers new hope to people who are ignored by the old financial system.

Bridging the Digital Divide

Despite everything good we've said, blockchain's potential means nothing if people can't access it.

Why is that the case?

- Internet access is still a luxury in many regions of the world.
- Crypto can be complicated. You've even had to read an entire book to understand. Is it any wonder many people don't know how to use it yet?

- Governments in some countries restrict access to crypto and blockchain technologies.

However, the good news is that solutions are emerging to address these problems.

For instance:

- Companies like **Blockstream** are working on satellite-powered blockchain transactions, meaning you won't need an internet connection to send crypto.
- Some companies are developing **low-cost smartphones with built-in blockchain wallets**, making crypto accessible in developing countries.
- Governments and NGOs are stepping in, helping communities understand how to use blockchain safely and effectively.

Had enough theory?

In the next chapter, we will have fun doing something practical.

Nothing complicated, though. We'll guide you through it.

Chapter 15

Web 3.0 Q & A – A Beginner's Guide

We have put down a few conceptual questions for your convenience and will answer them.

1. What is Web3?

Web3 or Web 3.0 is the next generation of the internet that is **decentralised, blockchain-based, and user-controlled**.

Features of Web3

- **Decentralised:** No central authority like Google or Facebook.
- **User-owned Data:** Users control their own information.
- **Uses Crypto Wallets:** Instead of traditional logins (e.g., MetaMask for authentication).

Examples of Web3 Applications

- **Brave Browser** – Rewards users with crypto for browsing.
- **Decentraland** – Virtual world owned by users.
- **ENS (Ethereum Name Service)** – Web3 domain names.

Analogy:

Web3 is like **an internet where users have full control instead of big corporations**.

2. What are Tokens and Coins?

Tokens and coins are both types of digital assets used in blockchain networks, but they have distinct differences.

Coins

A **coin** is a digital currency that operates on its own independent blockchain. It is mainly used as a **medium of exchange, store of value, and for network fees**.

Key Features:

- Has its own blockchain.
- Can be used for payments and transactions.
- Secures the network through mining or staking.

Examples:

- **Bitcoin (BTC)** – Digital gold, store of value.
- **Ethereum (ETH)** – Used to pay gas fees on Ethereum.
- **Solana (SOL)** – Used for transactions on the Solana blockchain.

Tokens

A **token** is a digital asset built on an existing blockchain and follows a specific token protocol (ERC-20, BEP-20, et cetera). Tokens are used for **smart contracts, governance, rewards, and decentralised finance (DeFi).**

Key Features:

- Built on top of another blockchain (e.g., ERC-20 tokens on Ethereum).

- Can represent assets, voting rights, access to services, or governance power.
- Requires the blockchain's native coin to pay for transactions.

Examples:

- **USDT (Tether)** – Stablecoin built on Ethereum (ERC-20).
- **Chainlink (LINK)** – Utility token for blockchain oracles.
- **AAVE (AAVE)** – Governance token for Aave lending protocol.

Analogy:

- A **coin** is like the **native currency of a country** (e.g., USD, EUR).
- A **token** is like a **gift card or loyalty points** that work within a specific system.

3. What is Crypto Mining?

Crypto mining is the process of validating transactions and adding them to the blockchain by solving complex mathematical problems.

How Mining Works

1. Miners compete to solve cryptographic puzzles (Proof of Work).
2. The first miner to solve the puzzle gets to add a block to the blockchain.
3. The miner is rewarded with new coins as an incentive.

Types of Mining

1. **Proof of Work (PoW)** – Uses computing power to solve puzzles (e.g., Bitcoin, Ethereum 1.0).
2. **Proof of Stake (PoS)** – Users stake coins to validate transactions instead of mining (e.g., Ethereum 2.0, Solana).
3. **Delegated Proof of Stake (DPoS)** – Users delegate their stake to validators (e.g., Binance Smart Chain).

Examples of Mining Coins

- **Bitcoin (BTC)**
- **Litecoin (LTC)**
- **Ethereum (before PoS upgrade)**

Analogy:

Mining is like **solving a Sudoku puzzle**—whoever solves it first wins the prize (newly minted coins).

4. What are Crypto Wallets?

A **crypto wallet** is a digital tool that allows you to store, send, and receive cryptocurrencies.

Types of Wallets

1. **Hot Wallets (Online)**
    - Connected to the internet, easier to use but less secure.
    - **Examples:** MetaMask, Trust Wallet, Coinbase Wallet.

2. **Cold Wallets (Offline)**
    - Stored on a physical device, highly secure but less convenient.

    Examples: Ledger Nano X, Trezor.
3. **Custodial Wallets**
    - Third parties manage your private keys (e.g., exchange wallets like Binance, Coinbase).
4. **Non-Custodial Wallets**
    - You control your private keys (e.g., MetaMask, Phantom).

Analogy:

- A **hot wallet** is like a **debit card**—easy to use but vulnerable to hacking.
- A **cold wallet** is like a **safe**—very secure but less convenient.

5. What is a Smart Contract?

A **smart contract** is a self-executing contract with terms written into code that runs on a blockchain.

How It Works

- Once predefined conditions are met, the contract executes automatically.
- No need for intermediaries (e.g., lawyers, banks).

Use Cases

- **DeFi (Decentralised Finance)** – Enables lending, staking, and trading without intermediaries.
- **NFTs (Non-Fungible Tokens)** – Smart contracts power ownership and transactions.

- **Gaming** – Enables in-game purchases and digital assets.

Example: A vending machine is like a smart contract: you insert money, and it automatically delivers the selected product.

6. What is Staking?

Staking is the process of locking up cryptocurrencies to help secure a blockchain network and earn rewards.

How It Works

1. Users **stake** (lock) their coins in a blockchain network.
2. They **become validators** (or delegate to a validator).
3. Validators **process transactions and maintain security**.
4. Stakers **earn rewards** in the form of new coins.

Examples:

- **Ethereum (ETH)**
- **Cardano (ADA)**
- **Solana (SOL)**
- **Polkadot (DOT)**

Analogy:
Staking is like **earning interest on a fixed deposit** in a bank.

7. What are NFTs (Non-Fungible Tokens)?

An **NFT (Non-Fungible Token)** is a unique digital asset that represents ownership of a specific item, such as art, music, or virtual land.

Key Features

- **Unique:** No two NFTs are identical.
- **Verifiable Ownership:** Stored on a blockchain.
- **Interoperable:** Can be traded across different platforms.

Examples

- **CryptoPunks** – Early digital collectibles.
- **Bored Ape Yacht Club (BAYC)** – Exclusive NFT collection.
- **Decentraland** – Virtual real estate in the Metaverse.

Analogy:

NFTs are like **digital baseball cards**—each one is unique and valuable.

8. What is DeFi (Decentralised Finance)?

DeFi refers to financial applications built on blockchain that operate **without banks or intermediaries**.

Key Features

- **Open and Permissionless:** Anyone can participate.
- **No Middlemen:** Transactions are automated using smart contracts.
- **Transparent:** All transactions are visible on the blockchain.

Examples

- **Uniswap** – Decentralised exchange (DEX).
- **Aave** – Crypto lending and borrowing.
- **Curve Finance** – Stablecoin liquidity pools.

Analogy:

DeFi is like **a bank that runs entirely on code instead of people**.

9. What is a Blockchain Protocol?

A **blockchain protocol** is the fundamental set of rules that govern a blockchain network. It defines how transactions are validated, how blocks are created, and how consensus is reached among network participants.

Key Features

Consensus Mechanism: Determines how transactions are verified (e.g., Proof of Work, Proof of Stake).

Security and Governance: Protects against fraud and ensures decentralised decision-making.

Smart Contracts: Enables automated execution of agreements.

Examples of Blockchain Protocols

Bitcoin (BTC) Protocol – Uses Proof of Work (PoW) for security.

Ethereum (ETH) Protocol – Uses Proof of Stake (PoS) and supports smart contracts.

Solana (SOL) Protocol – Uses Proof of History (PoH) for faster transactions.

Binance Smart Chain (BSC) – Offers low-cost, fast transactions for DApps.

Polkadot (DOT) Protocol – Enables multiple blockchains to connect.

10. What is a Token Protocol and How is It Different from a Blockchain Protocol?

A token protocol is a set of rules and standards that define how tokens function on a blockchain. While blockchain protocols govern the network itself, token protocols operate within a blockchain to manage digital assets.

Key Differences:

Feature	Blockchain Protocol	Token Protocol
Definition	Governs how the blockchain works	Governs how tokens operate on the blockchain
Function	Handles transactions, security, and decentralisation	Manages token supply, transfer, and interactions
Consensus Mechanism	Has its own mechanism (PoW, PoS, PoH)	Relies on the blockchain's mechanism
Examples	Bitcoin, Ethereum, Solana	ERC-20, ERC-721, SPL, BEP-20

Examples of Token Protocols

- **ERC-20 (Ethereum)** – Standard for fungible tokens (USDT, UNI, LINK).
- **ERC-721 (Ethereum)** – Standard for NFTs (CryptoPunks, Bored Apes).
- **BEP-20 (Binance Smart Chain)** – Equivalent of ERC-20 for BSC.
- **SPL (Solana)** – Token standard for Solana-based assets.

Analogy

- A blockchain protocol is like an operating system (Windows, macOS).
- A token protocol is like a software application (Microsoft Word, Photoshop) that runs on the OS.

11. What are the Layers of Blockchain?

Blockchain technology is structured into multiple layers to improve efficiency, scalability, and security.

Layer 0: Infrastructure Layer (Foundation)

- Provides the base infrastructure for blockchain networks.
- Enables multiple Layer 1 blockchains to connect.
- Examples: Polkadot Relay Chain, Cosmos IBC.

Layer 1: Base Blockchain (Consensus & Execution Layer)

- The main blockchain where transactions are validated.
- Uses consensus mechanisms like PoW, PoS.
- Examples: Bitcoin, Ethereum, Solana, Binance Smart Chain.

Layer 2: Scaling & Off-Chain Solutions

- Improves blockchain performance by processing transactions off-chain.
- Uses rollups, sidechains, and state channels.
- Examples: Lightning Network (Bitcoin), Arbitrum, Optimism, Polygon.

Layer 3: Application Layer (DApps & Smart Contracts)

- The user-facing layer that includes decentralised applications.

- Examples: Uniswap, OpenSea, Aave, Axie Infinity.

Layer 4: User Interaction & Services

- Includes wallets, oracles, and interoperability tools.
- Examples: MetaMask, Chainlink, Binance Bridge.

12. Why is Layer 0 Needed if we Already Have Solana, Avalanche, Ethereum, and Binance?

While Layer 1 blockchains like Ethereum, Solana, and Avalanche provide smart contract functionality, they lack interoperability, scalability, and flexibility. Layer 0 solves these issues by:

1. Connecting multiple blockchains – Reduces silos.
2. Improving scalability – Prevents congestion.
3. Allowing full customisation of Layer 1 chains – Developers can design unique features.
4. Providing shared security – New chains don't need to bootstrap security from scratch.

Top Layer 0 Blockchains:

Layer 0	Key Feature	Example Layer 1s Built on It
Polkadot (DOT)	Parachains & shared security	Moonbeam, Astar, Acala
Cosmos (ATOM)	Inter-Blockchain Communication (IBC)	Terra (before collapse), Cronos
Avalanche (AVAX)	Subnets for custom Layer 1s	Trader Joe, BenQi
Near Protocol (NEAR)	Sharding for scalability	Aurora, Octopus

13. Is There a Token Protocol That Fixes the Value of a Product Regardless of Token Fluctuations?

Yes! Several token mechanisms help fix the value of a product even if the price of a cryptocurrency fluctuates.

Stablecoin-Pegged Pricing

- Uses USDT, USDC, or DAI to fix the price of a product.
- If a user pays in a volatile token, it is converted into a stablecoin.

Time-Locked Price Stability

- A smart contract locks the price for a duration to prevent fluctuations.
- Uses oracles (e.g., Chainlink) to fetch exchange rates.

Dual-Token Model

- One token remains stable while the other fluctuates.
- Example: MakerDAO (DAI) uses volatile ETH as collateral but issues a stable DAI.

Rebasing Tokens (Elastic Supply)

- Expands/contracts supply to maintain a fixed value.
- Example: Ampleforth (AMPL) adjusts supply daily.

Futures and Hedging Contracts

- Locks in a fixed price using derivatives.
- Example: Synthetix (SNX) offers synthetic assets with stable value.

Fixed Exchange Rate via AMM

- Uses an Automated Market Maker (AMM) to maintain a stable rate.
- Example: Celo Dollar (cUSD) keeps a 1:1 peg to USD.

Method	How It Works	Best For
Stablecoin Pegging	Fixes price in USDT/ DAI	Crypto payments, e-commerce
Time-Locked Price Contracts	Locks price during transaction	ICOs, NFTs, Pre-sales
Dual-Token Model	One token is stable, the other fluctuates	Gaming, governance tokens
Rebasing Tokens	Adjusts supply to maintain value	Algorithmic stablecoins
Hedging Contracts	Uses futures for price stability	Institutional investors
Fixed AMM Rate	AMM controls price fluctuations	Lending, DeFi

Chapter 16

Developer's Guide to building DApps on Blockchain

What's an easy way to participate in the crypto and blockchain revolution that is upon us?

Buying crypto is one way to do that. But we already saw how simple it is to do that.

And what if you'd like to get more hands-on?

In that case, you might wish to create an app. Perhaps you could become a key service provider like Uniswap, Cryptokitties, or Aave.

And while the idea might sound terrifying, you can make it much more doable by breaking it down.

So, let's do that:

Step 1: Choose Your Blockchain

Not all blockchains out there are ideal for building DApps. Most developers out there are relying on the following:

- **Ethereum** is the most popular one, mainly thanks to smart contracts.

- **Binance Smart Chain (BSC)** – Faster and cheaper than Ethereum, but slightly more centralised.
- **Solana** is known for its speed and low fees. It's excellent for high-performance apps.

We'll use Ethereum for this guide since it's the most beginner-friendly.

Step 2: Write a Smart Contract

A smart contract is the heart of any DApp—it makes everything trustless and decentralised.

We'll write a simple Ethereum smart contract using Solidity, Ethereum's most common programming language.

But before we jump into the act, make sure you have the following tools:

1. Remix IDE

Writing code is easier when you have a tool built for the job. You can't just use Microsoft Word or Notepad.

An **Integrated Development Environment (IDE)** is what you'll need. An IDE typically packs a code editor and compiler into one tool, making life easy.

Now, there are IDEs you can download, but why bother to do that when you can access one already built for free online?

Remix IDE is one such tool; you can access it for freeat *https://remix.ethereum.org/* .

Besides being just a code editor and compiler, Remix also features a built-in **Ethereum Virtual Machine (EVM)** for testing, error detection, and debugging.

2. MetaMask

MetaMask functions as both a crypto wallet and a gateway to blockchain applications.

In that sense, it can offer the following features to DApp developers:

- Provide a bridge between your browser and the Ethereum blockchain.
- Allow you to sign transactions and interact with smart contracts.
- Allow you to use it on test networks, so you don't risk real money when developing.

In our case, you'll use MetaMask by downloading and installing its browser extension from *https://metamask.io*. There's an option for whatever browser you may be using.

After that, you'll definitely need…

3. A Test Network

Remember, you can't develop on the real Ethereum platform.

That's just too crazy because you'll always be making mistakes when developing and testing and transactions cost **gas fees**.

Test networks like **Goerli**, **Sepolia**, or **Rinkeby** are more suitable for the job.

We're especially fond of Goerli because you can visit their faucet *(https://www.alchemy.com/faucets/ethereum-sepolia)*, which is basically a free ETH dispenser, and load it up with test coins to use in development.

After you have something that works, you can deploy your app to the real **Ethereum** network.

The Solidity Language

Solidity is the language used to write smart contracts on the Ethereum platform. Many programmers feel that it's quite similar to Python or Javascript.

If you have experience with those two languages, you'll find that learning solidity isn't that difficult.

But, even if you've never programmed, you can still learn how to code from scratch in that language.

And many resources are available online for anyone who wants to learn Solidity. A personal favourite is this one over at *https://certify.northcard.org/blockchain*. You'll learn everything from the basics to advanced concepts.

For now, we'll ask you to open a new file and write the following code.

Example: A Simple Smart Contract

```
solidity
// SPDX-License-Identifier: MIT
pragma solidity ^0.8.0;
contract HelloBlockchain {
    string public message;

    constructor() {
        message = "Hello, Blockchain!";
    }
        function updateMessage(string memory
newMessage) public {
        message = newMessage;
    }
}
```

You probably wonder what this code is and what it's supposed to do.

First, understand that this is just a simple smart contract that stores a message on the blockchain and allows users to update it.

Now, let us break it down for you bit by bit.

The License and Version

```
solidity

// SPDX-License-Identifier: MIT

pragma solidity ^0.8.0;
```

This first snippet does nothing but inform other people who choose to read the code of the version of Solidity that was used. In this case, the version is **0.8.0**.

Declaring a Smart Contract

```
contract HelloBlockchain {
```

The following code snippet does nothing but define the smart contract. In other words, it gives this smart contract a name called **HelloBlockchain**.

The word ***contract*** is just a keyword that the Solidity language uses to define the contract name.

State Variable

```
string public message;
```

A variable is a container for storing a piece of data.

In this case, the keyword ***string*** tells Solidity that we are about to define a variable that will store test data.

Public is a scope declaration that tells the Solidity engine that every function in the code can read this variable.

Then ***message*** is simply the name of the variable itself.

Constructor Function

```
constructor() {
        message = "Hello, Blockchain!";
```

A **constructor function** is a piece of code that will run just **once** after the code has been deployed to a blockchain.

In this case, the code simply stores the string "Hello, Blockchain!" in the ***message*** variable.

A Function to Change the Message

```
        function  updateMessage(string  memory
newMessage) public {
        message = newMessage;
    }
```

A **function** is a block of instructions that can be called and executed at any instance in a code.

Beginning with the keyword ***function*** tells Solidity we are about to define a function. **updateMessage** is simply the name of the function itself.

It's a good practice to name functions according to what they do because it makes reading and understanding a piece of code easier. In this case, the function has been named **updateMessage** because that is what it does - update the variable called ***message***.

You'll also note the code within the parentheses. That place is reserved for the parameters of the function. Parameters are variables that are passed to a function at run-time.

In this case, the declaration **string memory newMessage** means that the function will take a text message as input as it runs and store it in the variable called **newMessage**.

The keyword ***public*** tells Solidity we can call this function at any point in the code.

Then the statement ***message = newMessage***; simply tells solidity to change the text stored within the message variable to whatever will be passed to the ***newMessage*** variable when the function is called.

So, basically, this smart contract works in a DApp like this:

- A user visits a webpage that interacts with this smart contract and views the already stored message. In this case, it's simply "Hello, Blockchain!"
- Afterward, they call the function updateMessage() to send a new message to the contract. This transaction is forever recorded.
- Anyone can view that webpage and see the latest message on the contract.

How sweet, right?

Save the file as **HelloBlockchain.sol**, and that's it.

Now, it's just a matter of deploying this code to a test network and connecting it to a front end.

But that's what steps three and four are for, so let's get to them quickly.

Step 3: Deploy Your Contract to a Test Network

Deploying your contract to a network makes it lie so people can run and use it.

But when actively developing the DApp, it's foolish to use the Ethereum mainnet because actions like those cost gas fees.

We've already established that Goerli is the testnet we recommend to beginners like you.

So, how do you go about deploying to it?

First, go to a Goerli faucet like Alchemy and load up your MetaMask wallet with ETH.

Then follow these steps:

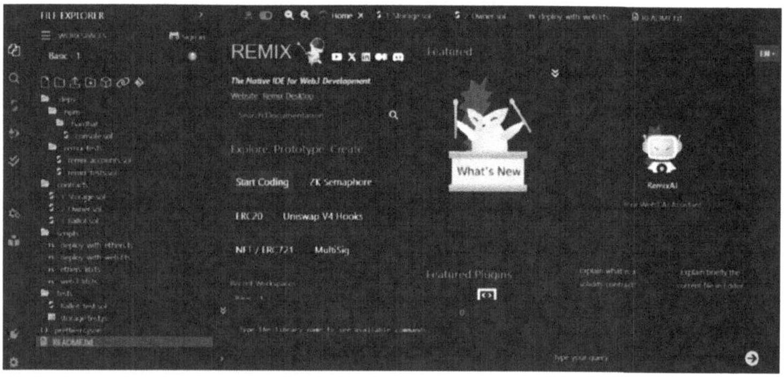

Figure 1. Remix IDE

- **Step 1: Open Remix** and paste your Solidity code in a new file.
- **Step 2: Compile the contract**

  Go to the "Solidity Compiler" tab (left panel). Click **Compile HelloBlockchain.sol** (make sure there are no errors).
- **Step 3: Connect MetaMask to Remix**

Go to the "Deploy & Run Transactions"tab.

Under **Environment**, select **Injected Provider - MetaMask.**

MetaMask will pop up—click **Confirm** to connect.

- **Step 4: Deploy to Goerli Testnet**

  Select your contract from the dropdown.

  Click **Deploy** and confirm the MetaMask transaction.

And that's it. Your precious contract is live on the **Goerli Testnet**.

Remix will show a transaction link to view your deployed contract. Click on it, and it will take you to **Etherscan for Goerli**, where you can view your contact address and transaction details and interact with them.

Now, it's just a matter of calling your contract's functions and writing a simple fronted interface to interact with it.

Step 4: Build the Frontend (User Interface)

A smart contract is great, but without an interface, users won't be able to interact with it.

So what do you do?

Two things:

- First, you'll need to use **HTML**, **CSS**, and **JavaScript** to code the interface like a standard web app.
- Then, you'll have to use **Web3.js** or **Ethers.js**. These are javascript libraries that let your website talk to the blockchain.

We can't teach you everything we've just outlined above. You'll have to do that yourself. The beautiful thing is that coding knowledge is plentiful on the internet right now.

You can learn everything you want. You just have to Google your problem, and you'll find a resource to help you.

Here's simple JavaScript code that connects a webpage to your smart contract.

```
javascript

const ethers = require("ethers");

const contractAddress = "YOUR_CONTRACT_ADDRESS_
HERE";

const abi = [ /* Your contract's ABI here */ ];

async function getMessage() {

    const provider = new ethers.providers.
Web3Provider(window.ethereum);

        const contract = new ethers.
Contract(contractAddress, abi, provider);


  const message = await contract.message();

  console.log("Blockchain Message:", message);

}
```

Essentially, this script does three things:

- Connects your website to Ethereum.
- Reads the message stored in your smart contract.
- Logs it in the browser console.

Step 5: Test, Improve, and Launch

Programmers rarely get it right on their first try.

It's usually a matter of testing and improving whatever you come up with until you have something that makes you and others happy.

So:

- Test everything – Use the testnet to find and fix bugs.
- Improve the user interface to make it more user-friendly.
- Once everything works, deploy your DApp on Ethereum Mainnet for real users!

Building a simple DApp isn't rocket science.

You've just learned the basics of blockchain development. You now know how to write, deploy, and connect a smart contract.

We know it looks intimidating at first. After all, you've probably struggled with the contents of this chapter alone.

But if you want to learn, you can venture out there and discover all you need to know about coding DApps.

And perhaps one day, you'll design something that matters.

Maybe you'll create something like a decentralised voting app, for instance? A simple NFT marketplace? We leave it all to your imagination.

Two Cents!

Money has always been about trust.

A piece of paper, a coin, or a digital number in your bank account all hold value because we *believe* they do. Cryptocurrency is no different. It challenges our old systems, questions who holds power, and redefines trust itself.

But beyond the technology and the hype, crypto is about something much bigger: **freedom.**

It's the freedom to send money across borders without permission.
It's the freedom to own assets that no bank, government, or institution can seize.
It's the freedom to innovate, to create something that reshapes the world.

The road ahead won't be easy. There will be failures, scams, and cycles of boom and bust. Some people will call it a bubble. Others will dismiss it as a fad. But remember—every major shift in history was once met with scepticism.

Think about the internet in the 90s. Many dismissed it as a playground for hobbyists. Today, it powers the world. Blockchain and crypto are following a similar path, but what happens next **depends on us.**

Will we build a system that is fairer, more open, and truly decentralised? Or will we allow greed, speculation, and bad actors to corrupt its potential?

That choice is ours to make.

Take your time, learn, and question everything. But don't just stand on the sidelines. Whether you're an investor, a developer, or simply someone curious about the future, your role in this revolution matters.

The next chapter of money is unwritten. And maybe—just maybe—*you* will be the one to write it.

Glossary of Key Terms

Before we part ways, let's break down some terms you've come across in this book and others that you are bound to hear in the crypto world:

A

- **Altcoin** – Any cryptocurrency **other than Bitcoin** (e.g., Ethereum, Solana, Cardano).
- **Airdrop** – Free crypto sent to your wallet (usually for marketing or as a reward).
- **ASIC (Application-Specific Integrated Circuit)** is a super-powerful computer built for crypto mining.

B

- **Blockchain** – A digital **ledger** that records transactions securely across a **network of computers**.
- **Bitcoin (BTC)** – The first and most well-known **cryptocurrency**, created by Satoshi Nakamoto in 2009.
- **Burning** – **Permanently removing coins** from circulation to reduce supply.

C

- **Crypto Wallet** – A digital **tool to store and manage** your cryptocurrencies.
- **Hot Wallet** – Online and connected to the internet (e.g., MetaMask, Trust Wallet).

- **Cold Wallet** – Offline storage for security (e.g., Ledger, Trezor).
- **CBDC (Central Bank Digital Currency)** – A digital version of a national currency issued by a government.
- **Consensus Mechanism** – The method used to **verify transactions** on a blockchain (e.g., Proof of Work, Proof of Stake).

D

- **DApp (Decentralised Application)** – An app that runs **on a blockchain**, not a central server.
- **DeFi (Decentralised Finance)** – Financial services (loans, savings, trading) that operate **without banks**.
- **DAO (Decentralised Autonomous Organisation)** – A blockchain-based community that makes decisions **without a CEO**.

E

- **Ethereum (ETH)** – The second-largest cryptocurrency, known for **smart contracts** and **DApps**.
- **Etherscan** – A website to **track Ethereum transactions** and smart contracts.

F

- **Fiat Currency** – Government-issued money like the **US Dollar ($)** or **Euro (€)**.
- **Fork** – A change to a blockchain's rules, creating a **new version** (e.g., Bitcoin vs. Bitcoin Cash).
- **FOMO (Fear of Missing Out)** – The feeling of rushing to buy crypto before it skyrockets.

G

- **Gas Fees** – The cost of making transactions on a blockchain (mainly Ethereum).
- **Genesis Block** – The very **first block** of a blockchain.

H

- **HODL** – A misspelled "hold" that became crypto slang for **holding onto coins long-term**.
- **Halving** – A Bitcoin event that **cuts mining rewards in half**, reducing new BTC supply.

I

- **ICO (Initial Coin Offering)** – A way for crypto projects to **raise funds** by selling new tokens.
- **Interoperability** – The ability of **different blockchains to communicate** and share data.

L

- **Layer 2 Solution** – A tech upgrade that makes **blockchains faster and cheaper** (e.g., Lightning Network, Polygon).
- **Liquidity** – How **easily** you can buy or sell a cryptocurrency **without affecting the price**.

M

- **Mining** – The process of **validating blockchain transactions** and earning rewards.
- **Market Cap** – The total value of a cryptocurrency (**price × supply**).

N

- **NFT (Non-Fungible Token)** – A **unique digital asset** representing art, music, or collectibles.
- **Node** – A computer that helps **maintain a blockchain network**.

P

- **Private Key** – A secret password that lets you **control your crypto** (NEVER share this!).
- **Proof of Work (PoW)** – A security method where miners solve **complex puzzles** (used by Bitcoin).
- **Proof of Stake (PoS)** – A newer, energy-efficient way to **validate transactions** (used by Ethereum 2.0).

S

- **Smart Contract** – A self-executing program that runs **on a blockchain** (no middlemen needed).
- **Stablecoin** – A crypto tied to a **stable asset** like the US Dollar (e.g., USDT, USDC).
- **Scam Coins** – Fake or shady cryptocurrencies created to **steal money**.

T

- **Token** – A digital asset **built on an existing blockchain** (e.g., ERC-20 tokens on Ethereum).
- **Testnet** – A **fake blockchain** used for testing before launching on the real network.
- **Transaction Hash (TXID)** – A unique **ID number** for every blockchain transaction.

W

- **Web3** – The **next generation of the internet**, built on blockchain and decentralisation.
- **Whale** – Someone who holds **a massive amount** of crypto, enough to move markets.

Y

- **Yield Farming** – Earning passive income by **lending or staking crypto**.

Other Books by the Authors